Merry Christmas
to
Mother
with our love,
Janice and Gor...
12/25/2000

☆ see page 119

HISTORIC ABILENE

An Illustrated History

by Tracy M. Shilcutt, David Coffey & Donald S. Frazier

Published for the Abilene Preservation League

Historical Publishing Network
A division of Lammert Publications, Inc.
San Antonio, Texas

CONTENTS

First Edition

Copyright © 2000 Historical Publishing Network

All rights reserved. No part of this book may be reproduced in any form or by any means, electronic or mechanical, including photocopying, without permission in writing from the publisher. All inquiries should be addressed to Historical Publishing Network, 8491 Leslie Road, San Antonio, Texas, 78254. Phone (210) 688-9008.

ISBN: 1-893619-06-0
Library of Congress Card Catalog Number: 00-102629

Historic Abilene: An Illustrated History

authors:	Tracy M. Shilcutt
	David Coffey
	Donald S. Frazier
cover design:	Blaine Reid
contributing writer for "sharing the heritage":	Johnnye Montgomery

Historical Publishing Network

president:	Ron Lammert
vice president:	Barry Black
project manager:	Joe Neely
director of operations:	Charles A. Newton, III
administration:	Angela Lake
	Donna Mata
	Dee Steidle
graphic production:	Colin Hart
	John Barr

PRINTED IN SINGAPORE

ACKNOWLEDGMENTS

Bryan Shilcutt, Erin Shilcutt, Jackie Beth Shilcutt, Geoff Gilbert, Kathy Aldridge, Ruby Perez and the Abilene Preservation League, Jana Smith and the Grace Museum, Amber McClendon, B. W. Aston and the Abilene Historical Photographic Collection at Hardin-Simmons University, Abilene Chamber of Commerce, Vernon Williams and the Twelfth Armored Division Memorial Museum, and Lisa Wiggins. Bill Whitaker and the *Abilene Reporter-News*, Joe Specht and the staff at McMurry University's Jay-Rollins Library, Alice Specht and the staff of the Hardin-Simmons University Libraries, Brandon Polk, Lisa Sanders, Tom Perini, Lawrence Clayton, Nanci Liles, and Charlie Dromgoole.

Looking south down Pine Street, c. 1925.

COURTESY ABILENE PRESERVATION LEAGUE.

FOREWORD

A decade or so ago, Abilene Chamber of Commerce officials—ever seeking the magic slogan to lure people from far and beyond to this Lone Star city of more than 100,000—hatched a whole new campaign. For the rest of the twentieth century, they began summing up Abilene as, simply, "A Whole Lotta Texas Goin' On." Done up in a striking logo with vibrant colors featuring flowering cacti and beet-red sun, the slogan was a spirited, upbeat one, even if the claim seemed curiously out of step with the town's past. Abilene, for instance, never firmly established itself as the bustling cattle town its founders envisioned (to the extent those same founders named the place after a rip-roaring cattle town in Kansas, thereby creating more than a century of confusion for tourists, historians, and trivia-game competitors). Nor did it ever evolve into a historically significant hub during the periodic oil booms that seized other parts of Texas (though chamber officials did drill for oil as an inspired publicity stunt during the town's 1981 centennial—and, to everyone's surprise, even struck oil).

Unlike historic Fort Griffin, an hour's drive north, Abilene never exploded into so much as an intriguing footnote in Wild West annals (though local students routinely learn about two rival newspaper editors "dueling" on the dusty streets of early-day Abilene— a bone-headed farce in which they ultimately heaped more humiliation upon themselves than committing serious injury to each other). And while its military heritage has provided the town with much of its color, even its beginnings in this regard were undistinguished. Nearby Fort Phantom Hill was abandoned only a few years after its 1851 construction following an inspector's report that the area was fit for neither man nor beast—a notion even some nomadic Indians in this stretch of the Southwest tended to agree with. That may be one reason why no historically significant, truly hair-raising battles between Indians and the Army ever took place in these parts. Indeed, the wildest this bit of West Texas likely ever got—at least in the conventional sense of the American West—was when various and sundry Wild West shows stopped temporarily in the area to show local folks how it was really done.

Judging from some accounts, Pearl Beer, Farrah Fawcett, Frito-Lay, and horny toads have all had more to do with the cultural make-up of Texas than Abilene. And perhaps such accounts are right. Abilene has always been an enigma, now more than ever, both to outsiders and itself. Townfolks can't even agree exactly where it is. At one point in the 1990s, some area boosters took to referring to the Abilene area as the "Texas Midwest," which in terms of geographic location and what passes for midwestern attitudes is absolutely correct. Others more deeply rooted to the area, however, saw this as a transparent gesture to deny the truth—that Abilene is, first and foremost, an integral part of West Texas. Over the years, I've met many in this area who have continually and strenuously denied Abilene is in West Texas, partially because of all the prickly connotations of barren stretches and wandering tumbleweeds and western diamondbacks the very term "West Texas" seems to conjure up. But other individuals close to this sun-baked, alkaline soil take special pride in living in West Texas, if only because their day-to-day existence in such a seemingly inhospitable land quietly says something about their own determination, hardiness and faith.

Abilene has always seemed a place in search of an identity, beginning with its origins as a wind-blown railroad town, set up by Texas & Pacific administrators in coldly methodical, by-the-book fashion. And if being stuck with the copycat name of Abilene weren't hindrance enough, the young town had to bear the additional burden of a nickname given it by early-day town promoters—the "Future Great City of West Texas"—a rather presumptuous bit of self-importance that brought rib-tickling derision from other towns and their newspapers, if it brought any comment at all. As the years progressed, the pre-ordained title "Future Great City of West Texas" dropped from the lexicon of Abilenians, but the town's given name of Abilene continued to create confusion. At least, it wasn't as confusing as what happened just several miles down the T&P Railway tracks, where an engineer accidentally dropped off the wrong signs in the budding towns of Eskota and Trent. In the end, what was supposed to be Trent but instead became Eskota dwindled into what passed for a ghost town, while what was supposed to be Eskota but instead became Trent stubbornly stuck it out as a town of about 300 by the end of the twentieth century. Of course, that too was enough for haughty big-city types to brand it a ghost town.

Meanwhile, Abilene has quietly prospered into a city of more than 100,000. Much of its character, for better or worse, has come from the three religiously oriented colleges that blossomed into universities. The mightiest of these is Abilene Christian University, an upwardly mobile Church of Christ institution already on high ground and very much, as ACU historian and Chancellor Emeritus Dr. John C. Stevens put it in his recent history on the university, "a city set on a hill." And yet, the straight and narrow Abilene Christian University might not have taken root in what some call "God's country" had founder A. B. Barret not deemed the water in nearby Ballinger downright ungodly in taste. He also took offense in San Angelo after the wind blew his hat off and city fathers meeting with him frowned upon the mere cap he replaced it with. Just down the street from ACU is Hardin-Simmons University, a Baptist institution with a strict tradition, yet a mischievous sense of humor where, among other things, a favorite campus dog is buried, its name—"Dam-it"—proudly etched on a stone marker in the heart of the campus. As for McMurry University, a Methodist institution, the atmosphere has been considerably looser, to the point that, during the dance-happy 1970s, students from ACU and HSU—long preached to about the evils of dancing— simply traveled across town to attend the campus dances at McMurry. At one point, McMurry officials implemented a rule that only students with McMurry ID cards would be admitted to campus dances, thus calming complaints by sufficiently outraged university officials at ACU and HSU and also allowing McMurry students and their dates a bit more space to get footloose.

Abilene also sees itself as patriotic, partially because of its military heritage. Savvy to the economic prospects involved, Abilene campaigned for a huge Army training camp southwest of town on the eve of America's involvement in World War II, then spent most of the war courting the tens of thousands of soldiers themselves. With Abilene just emerging from the trials of the Great Depression, city fathers spoke of Camp Barkeley as the town's salvation, though the camp also went a ways toward highlighting Abilene's occasional hypocrisy. Abilene was officially "dry" when it came to demon rum, but visiting soldier boys could still procure "medicinal alcohol" at local pharmacies. Men from the nearby Army camp also romanced many of the local girls, to the degree that even most of the old maids in Abilene got married off before the camp's closure in 1945. Inspired by the many benefits to having the military in town, city fathers soon began working to land a more permanent military installation following World War II, their efforts being rewarded when Dyess Air Force Base opened near Abilene in the thick of the Cold War. Among other things, the base became the first home of the B-1 bomber, whose sole original purpose was to stealthily deliver the doomsday bomb if and when the situation threatened. Right up until the collapse of the Soviet Union and even afterward, Abilenians have never seemed to mind living in what no doubt became one of the top nuclear targets, though some area ranchers have occasionally expressed concern about low-level training missions disrupting the tranquil life of their cattle.

But if Abilenians' sense of themselves and their place in the grand scheme of things still seems vague, the situation is due at least in part to the relative neglect they've given their own past. In the often rambunctious oil-drilling days during the final third of the twentieth century, Abilene was concerned more about where it was headed than where it had been. This proved particularly so during the oil boom days of the 1970s and early '80s, when waves of people poured into the area seeking easy prosperity and everyone devoted their leisure hours to reveling in this hard land rather than worrying about anything as insignificant as our pioneer past. Indeed, much of the recent restoration of historic buildings downtown—aided tremendously by the Abilene Preservation League—came about only after the boom had gone bust, the bottom dropped out of the oil market and the resources required to finance such undertakings proved far harder to come by. It's been that way with the town's history, too. When most academicians at the three local universities largely ignored Abilene's fast-fleeting history—the most notable exception being peerless Vernon Spence, who might have attempted a proper history of Abilene had he lived longer—the dusty trail was left to others to chronicle. Most significant among them was crusty, veteran *Reporter-News* Page One columnist Katharyn Duff, whose straightforward *Abilene…on Catclaw Creek* was first published by her employers in 1969, and freelance writer Juanita Zachry, who in 1986 took a break from compiling small-town histories to write a succinct history of Abilene in *Abilene: The Key City*. And then there is *A Personal Country*, a true classic by Texas historian, newspaperman, and Abilene native A. C. Greene, eloquently evoking the soul of this stretch of West Texas in a way no one else ever has.

The book in hand offers not only a fresh perspective on Abilene's history but a striking re-evaluation of past research by a new breed of historians—specifically, Tracy Shilcutt, David Coffey and Don Frazier of the aggressive Grady McWhiney Foundation now based at McMurry University. They are what I call "activist historians." Respectful of the trails blazed by earlier historians, they nevertheless have been reluctant to rely on the usual sources for past accounts and have charged after new ones, all while rethinking the standard interpretations of dusty, bygone days. In the process, they have furnished a dramatic, personally relevant history of Abilene that not only promises to stand as a sturdy reference for years to come but may even go a ways toward making us rethink ourselves as we head into the new millennium. And if this proper, yet visceral new history happens to come in the form of a fund-raiser for the Abilene Preservation League—well, I can't think of a better group it should be linked with. In many ways, the league's leadership has already seen the future—and much of it involves successfully playing upon our past.

If nothing else, this book should offer Abilenians a few more points of civic pride than those we already cling to. Over the years, such points of pride have routinely boiled down to Abilene's status as the very first city in all Texas to pass a half-cent sales tax for local economic development (not the sort of thing, frankly, that sets outsiders afire); its fame as home to the B-1 bomber (and there really are people who enjoy parking just beyond Dyess Air Force Base and watching the sleek bombers perform touch-and-go training exercises); its spicy distinction as the first city to ever have a Taco Bueno restaurant (though the Mexican fast-food chain finally abandoned its first restaurant in 1999 for a boxy new building, much to the sorrow of longtime patrons); and, finally, the fact the very institution of high school marching bands in Texas was begun at Abilene High School by "Prof" Raymond T. Bynum way back in 1926 (and, just for the record, curmudgeonly, ninety-four-year-old Prof Bynum conducted both Abilene and Cooper High School bands in what he claimed would be his final performance of *The Stars and Stripes Forever* during the Abilene Independent School District convocation in August 1999). Of course, each town has a particular notion of what things it should and should not be known for. Thanks to the new history at hand, at least now we'll have more to choose from.

Bill Whitaker,
Abilene Reporter-News

FOLSOM POINTS AND FREE RANGE

AN INTRODUCTION TO THE HISTORY OF ABILENE

The identity of the first human being to wander across the hills and prairies of what would eventually become Taylor County is lost to antiquity, but he likely arrived more than nine thousand years ago. He was a hunter, knapping oblong, fluted tips for his spears from loaves of flint near present-day Jim Ned Creek. He hunted dear, and bison, primitive camels, even the great wooly mammoth. He ate their flesh and wore their skins. Modern anthropologists have characterized him as part of the Folsom culture.

Generations of these people came and went. By 500 BC, the mammoths and giant bison were gone, as were the camels and horses. Gone, too, were the simple push spears, replaced by the more deadly atl-atl, a hand and shoulder operated spear launching lever that was, for its day, an absolute marvel of physics. With this device, humans had a distance weapon that could be used to ambush even the wariest of prey, including the American Bison, or buffalo. The projectile points from these devices litter the modern countryside, often erroneously referred to as "arrow heads." Around the turn of the first millennium, true bows and arrows, with their tiny stone tips, had replaced the bulky atl-atl, increasing the rate of success for these indigenous people, allowing their population to grow. Even so, by 1492 there were only about 1.5 million humans living between the Arctic Circle and the Rio Grande. Those living in present-day Taylor County were very few, but their kind had been here for nearly 300 generations.

When the Spanish arrived in Texas in the sixteenth and seventeenth centuries, they forever changed the lives of these original people. First of all, they named the human beings they found collectively as Indians; those living among the hills of the present-day Callahan Divide and among the valleys of the Brazos and Colorado Rivers specifically they dubbed "Jumanos." These traders moved by foot in those early, pre-horse days, staying close to water. They were religious folk, mining pigmented minerals from the hills and gullies of the region, and painting their mystical calling cards on the bluffs later called Paint Rock. The arrival of the Spanish, though, unleashed forces that would eventually overwhelm the peaceful Jumanos. Although Europeans explored the region, they found little of value to keep them interested; what they left behind would change the human landscape.

Spanish diseases, horses, and, eventually, guns began cycles of conquest. Death in the form of microbes stalked the Indian encampments, leading to huge social upheaval while weakening the peoples' ability to hunt and fight. Horse-borne raiders rode the Great Plains, freed from their old pedestrian limitations, following the seemingly endless supply of buffalo and attempting to monopolize trade with the Europeans. Ranges for hunting and trading parties now tripled, allowing the horse masters to roam farther from spring and creek. Surprise and shock, coupled with the power of firearms, became the new strategy as foreigners from the north displaced the peoples who had lived in the area for centuries.

Like waves breaking upon the beach, groups and Indians invaded the region, driving out all the people in their path. By 1700, the Apaches, themselves refugees from invaders beyond the horizon, had overrun the Jumanos, pushing them south into the cultural anonymity of Mexico. The Apaches held sway until, they too, fell victim. By the 1780s, a rogue band of Shoshonis had splintered the Apaches into nearly a dozen bands, scattering them to the south and southwest. The Spanish identified these newcomers as Los Comanches and for a seven decades, these Indians dominated the southern Great Plains. Their numbers grew, and the most southerly of their immigrant groups, the Paneteka or "Honey Eaters," occasionally wandered the hills and valleys of present-day Taylor County, using it as a safe haven for their families while they raided into Mexico or hunted on the plains. But they, too, would be displaced—their sanctuary undone.

Nomadic Indians had lived a sporadic existence in the region, but invaders from the east would bring permanent residents to the area. The Spanish had gone, as had their heirs, the Mexicans.

This outstanding image shows cowboys from the Reynolds Cattle Company. Cattlemen such as John Simpson and the Merchant brothers were instrumental in establishing Abilene, which they named for the famous cattle-shipping Kansas railhead.
COURTESY THE ALBANY NEWS.

Texans, a seemingly new breed of men, began to make themselves known along the banks of the Brazos and the Colorado. The Comanches called them "the ones who always follow us home" in a backhanded homage to the persistence of these people, and eventually the pressure of the Texan raids broke the back of Paneteka supremacy. When Texas joined the United States, soldiers would begin a process that would bring permanent inhabitants to the area. U.S. troops established Fort Phantom Hill in 1851, Fort Chadbourne in 1852, Camp Colorado in 1856, and Camp Cooper in 1857. Although garrisons came and went, the prairies and hills they patrolled were no longer safe for Indians. They weren't entirely safe for white men, either. Still, in 1858 the Texas legislature created Taylor County, named for brothers Edward, James, and George Taylor, all killed at the Alamo.

The same resources that had lured the original peoples to the county also lured new immigrants. In 1873, hunters moved in, making their camps along Elm Creek in Buffalo Gap. Their forays onto the prairies to the north and south and into the hollows of the Callahan Divide allowed an unfettered look at the land and its resources, while spelling the doom of the Comanches as an independent people. By 1876, all of the Indians were gone, and the buffalo were going fast. Less transitory settlers arrived, including Sam Gholson, William C. Dunn, and

William E. Cureton, establishing the town of Buffalo Gap in 1878 and organizing a county government. Work on a permanent courthouse began early the next year.

Others came, too. Some pushed their beeves out onto the sea of grass, fattening them up on the free range before driving them to market. A few dozen miles to the east, in Callahan County, John and Claiborne "Clabe" Merchant established themselves in the cattle business. They had fought in the Civil War, having served with the Fourteenth Texas Cavalry, and like many cash-strapped post-war Texans they turned to driving cattle as a way to make their fortunes. The twins left their Nacogdoches homes and eventually established the 74 Ranch near the town of Belle Plain in 1874. Likewise, John Simpson, himself a veteran of the Fourth Tennessee Cavalry, made his "grubstake" trailing cattle through Weatherford, and took advantage of the vacant pasturage in Taylor County the following year. He brought in a herd of longhorns to begin the Hashknife Ranch, with his headquarters dugout on a bluff overlooking Cedar Creek in the northeast corner of the county.

A variety of other settlers moved in with various degrees of success. An enthusiastic band of Midwestern farmers established the Eagle Colony in the eastern part of the county, only to be overcome by the fickle climate. They lost their savings and their faith, and returned home. Other immigrants brought in sheep, but eventually moved

their operations further south. Bone pickers also arrived, mounding up great pyramids of sunbleached buffalo bones that would later be sold and ground for fertilizer or used as a bleaching agent for the Louisiana sugar industry. The abundance of buffalo carcasses on the plains led to a boom in the prairie wolf population, which were hunted to extinction by professionals willing to risk disfigurement or death for the hide bounties. When census takers arrived in 1880, they counted some 917 people living on 107 farms and ranches in Taylor County, along with 30,000 head of cattle and 6,000 head of sheep. Livestock dominated the economy; farmers raised only 157 acres of wheat and seventy-three acres of corn.

The railroad, though, dominated everyone's future plans. By 1880, it was obvious that a great change was about to sweep West Texas. Boosters of Buffalo Gap looked eagerly toward the day when the Texas and Pacific Railroad, the long awaited southern railroad route across the continent, laid their tracks through the town, although this was in no way a sure thing. Speculation as to the final route, which would spell boom or bust for many a West Texas town, became a full-time occupation for many. Merchants and citizens in the fledgling communities started by cowmen and buffalo hunters assumed that the rails would logically follow the settlements.

Theirs was a false assumption based on a lack of appreciation for the transforming power of this steel-riding technology. More ambitious settlers realized that the coming of the railroad broke all carefully held assumptions about transportation routes and population centers. It would go where it pleased, and it often bypassed, and eventually killed, existing towns. Instead, a correct guess of the railroad route, with its power to transform the human geography of the region, was perhaps the biggest gamble of the settlers lives. Simply stated, it would make or break them. If clever land speculators and ambitious men could shorten the odds or predict with unerring accuracy of the final roadbed, then a fortune could be made in "town building."

In 1880, the great processes of history had been in play along the banks of Elm and Catclaw Creeks. Signs of the passing of humans abounded. From Clovis points to rifle shell casings, from buffalo bones to lonely pioneer outposts, the tides of human occupation had merely lapped at the hills of Taylor County. There had been little to keep large numbers of people there. That would soon change, and the railroad would be the agent of the next great phase in the history of the land and its people.

Above: Ox-drawn wagons haul buffalo hides in Taylor County, c. 1876.

Below: A typical buffalo skinning camp with hides stretched out and drying, c. 1876.
COURTESY TEXAS STATE ARCHIVES.

"THE FUTURE GREAT CITY OF WEST TEXAS"

Abilene's creation coincided with the Texas and Pacific Railway Company's race west in pursuit of government land grants. In the 1880s, the lure of land in the unsettled portions of West Texas attracted both the railroad and settlers in search of new beginnings. In 1881, visionary cattle ranchers and railroad speculators negotiated a compromise that put Milepost 407 on the map as the new town of Abilene. Together, they established a pattern of salesmanship and embellishment, promoting Abilene as "The Future Great City of West Texas." The T&P brought Abilene to life through exaggerated and idealized promotion, but determined citizens guaranteed the town's survival through their commitment to the vision of a great community.

THE TEXAS AND PACIFIC RAILWAY COMPANY AND THE CREATION OF THE WEST TEXAS CAPITAL

The Texas and Pacific Railway Company began operation in 1871, when Congress authorized a southern rail route to connect the state of Texas to the Pacific Ocean. Rail lines already extended to western Louisiana and within Texas, but no tracks crossed Texas borders. Although a northern transcontinental railroad was completed in 1869, the mountainous road proved challenging to travelers, who encountered hazardous conditions and unpredictable weather. The hot, dry climate of a southern route offered a more predictable journey for westbound homesteaders. It also linked the Lone Star State to the rest of the country.

Although a southern transcontinental route offered several benefits, investors were reluctant to gamble on a railroad through untamed and desolate territory. The United States government believed that incentives might help to lure investors, so Congress promised the railroad companies twenty to forty sections of public land for every mile of track laid from Texas to California. With this guarantee of investment return, the Texas and Pacific Railway Company surveyed the Southwest for the most direct route to the Pacific.

The T&P began construction in 1871 at Marshall, Texas. Although planners aimed toward El Paso, they had not yet determined the exact route the rail would take across the state. This soon became the least of their concerns as company financial problems and disease among work crews slowed construction. By 1880, the T&P extended no farther than Fort Worth. But that year, the railroad company came back to life under the leadership of railroad magnate Jay Gould. The pace picked up as the Texas and Pacific headed west once more.

While Gould reorganized the company, he relied on his chief engineer and the president of the T&P Construction Company, Grenville M. Dodge, to oversee day-to-day construction. Dodge, a Union general during the Civil War, pushed his crews toward El Paso, knowing the final location for the line was still undetermined. He understood that the financial rewards for the T&P could be enhanced if it by-passed existing towns, choosing instead to encourage new settlements. Dodge authorized townsite locators to travel ahead of the construction gang to find the best locations for new towns, which would by extension establish the route for the railroad.

Railroad representatives moved westward, sparking widespread rumors about the potential route and stirring excitement and speculation among pioneer residents. As news and gossip spread throughout West Texas, land speculators bought acreage in Callahan, Jones, and Taylor Counties. The two most sought after sites were Buffalo Gap, the Taylor County seat, and the area around old Fort Phantom Hill in Jones County. Local residents were not the only participants in these speculative activities. One railroad representative bought land in the Tebo (Tye) area, perhaps acting on insider information. The speculators' efforts went unrewarded as a self-appointed delegation opted for an entirely different location.

This early view looks west on the town. Cows and horses occasionally escaped their backyard confinement to roam the town's streets.

THE TEXAS & PACIFIC RY.

The group responsible for the location of the railtown included John Simpson, S. L. Chalk, John T. Berry, and brothers John and Clabe Merchant. They first met with a T&P representative at Simpson's Hashknife Ranch headquarters on Cedar Creek (just west of present Abilene Christian University) in the early fall of 1880 to consider three sites: Tye, Elmdale, or acreage on the Hashknife Ranch. Through a series of negotiations, the Hashknife group decided to locate the new town on acreage that included sections of the Hashknife Ranch and land just south-southwest of the Hashknife, between Cedar Creek and Big Elm Creek. The T&P marked the new townsite as Milepost 407, indicating that the town was 407 miles from the railroad's eastern terminus of Marshall. When railroad officials left the naming of the new town to locals, Clabe Merchant advanced the name of Abilene after Abilene, Kansas, hoping the town would become a great railhead.

The December 1880 contract between the railroad and the Hashknife group sized the new townsite at 1,760 acres and divided organizational responsibilities. Local landowners committed to build a permanent depot and cattle pens for the anticipated shipping industry, and the T&P committed to advertise and conduct a lot sale. The two parties further agreed to split the profits evenly. In preparation for the sale, T&P representatives staked out the town boundaries, specified lots to be sold, and settled locations for streets and alleys. According to early Abilenian H. A. Tillet, railroad man J. Stoddard Johnston numbered the east-west streets so that one could tell at a glance how far they were from the railroad. Johnston gave the north-south streets popular tree names in the hope that citizens would beautify the new town by planting that particular variety along the corresponding streets. The original town boundaries extended to North 7th Street, bounded by Cottonwood to Grape on the north side of the tracks, and to South 7th and Cherry to Poplar on the south side. With plans concisely formulated, the railroad began a vigorous campaign to introduce and sell the new town to the rest of the world.

In late December 1880, General Dodge invited a reporter from the *Dallas Herald* to visit Milepost 407. The men rode the train to the western terminus at Baird, then proceeded to the new site by horse. The reporter became the first to record the name "Abilene," when he provided a description of the new townsite in the December 23, 1880 edition of the *Herald*. Shortly thereafter, a propaganda campaign initiated by the T&P advertised the "Future Great City of West Texas," in the *Herald* and several East Texas newspapers. In February 1881, the *Herald* depicted the surrounding area as "level as a floor" and promoted the town's anticipated growth spurt that would follow the lot sale. The newspaper also speculated that Baird would become the town of more importance.

The *Herald* emphasized a need for building materials proved well founded, for even before the official ad campaign began scattered tents housed residents as well as businesses (this reportedly included saloons, gambling houses, and dance halls). Railroad construction crews extended the line into the community by mid-January 1881, but the first train did not steam in until February 27. On the same day that locals gathered to welcome the T&P engine, Presbyterian faithful established the town's first church—in a tent—instituting a moral aspect that would become an integral part of Abilenene's character, identity, and growth. But other early incidents were more characteristic of the wild and lawless West.

Just weeks before the first train arrived, a special correspondent for the *Herald* reported that the young frontier community had been shocked by the murder of a man named Snoddy. The sheriff arrested a Mr. Wright (Snoddy's partner), Wright's wife, and Wright's two sons-in-law for the murder. Suspicion fell upon Wright and his family because Wright, who was very poor, "suddenly" found several hundred dollars to spend on supplies. Rumors spread that

Snoddy had been on "intimate terms" with Wright's daughters. Authorities quickly released one of the sons-in-law, but what happened to the rest of the Wright clan went unrecorded. While the tent community's image might have been tarnished by this episode, an intensified newspaper ad campaign extolled the area's positive potential.

The railroad's imaginative promotional campaign described Abilene as a "garden spot of the state…destined to become one of the most important points" on the T&P line. The ads also announced the town lot sale scheduled for March 15, 1881, with the Fort Worth paper devoting front-page ads to the event for at least one week. Evidently the hype paid off, for just days before the sale the *Dallas Herald* reported that at least three hundred people lived in the "remarkably quiet" frontier town.

The day of the sale dawned cold, but weather did not prevent a crowd from gathering early around the auctioneer's block at South 1st and Chestnut. Resident tent dwellers waited to bid on land for permanent homes and businesses, and other eager investors came on a special five coach train that arrived at 4:00 a.m. on the 15th, just hours before the auction began. Estimates of the early morning crowd ranged from 800 to 2,000. As the auctioneer's gavel signaled the start of the sale, the railroad immediately sold two lots located on the northwest corner of Pine and North 2nd to John T. Berry

Theodore Heyck Shipping and Commission became one of the largest wool shipping businesses in Texas in the late nineteenth century. The Heyck warehouse was located at North 1st and Cypress.

for a total of $710. The *Herald* reported that
Berry's purchase ignited a flurry of bidding that
continued throughout the day and into the next.
Over the course of the two day auction, 178 lots
(both business and residential) sold for a total of
$27, 550. Abilene's future appeared secure with
the auction successfully completed, but that of
the T&P remained in question.

When Jay Gould took control of the Texas
and Pacific Railway Company, he faced fierce
competition in the race for El Paso, both to cap-
ture the wealth offered by Texas land grants and
to gain control of the line continuing west. C. P.
Huntington's Southern Pacific Railroad pushed
eastward from California to Texas and quickly
was approaching El Paso by the time the T&P
founded Abilene. T&P laborers steadily laid
about twelve miles of track per day, but it
became apparent that Huntington's line would
reach El Paso first. Gould would have to compromise to gain access to the western extension
of the rail. After arduous negotiations, Gould
and Huntington agreed that the Texas and

Pacific would halt construction about 100 miles
outside of El Paso at Sierra Blanca. There, the
two lines met on New Year's Day, 1882.

If the Texas and Pacific Railway Company's
ambitions to construct a railroad from Texas to
the Pacific were dashed when the Southern
Pacific reached El Paso first, the railroad's idealized campaign to promote "The Future Great
City of West Texas" became a resounding success. Abilene adopted this self-glorifying and
often exaggerated personality and resolved to
make the railroad's boast come true.

GROWTH OF THE "QUEEN CITY"

The Texas and Pacific established new towns
roughly every twenty miles along the rail line,
creating competition between communities as
each sought to attract newcomers to their site.
The frontier town of Abilene lay in the middle of
an expansive prairie, so while the railroad
offered transportation, there were few geographical benefits to encourage settlement. Abilene's
topography was so flat that the small range of the

Callahan Divide easily could be seen to the south, while from every other direction, the land appeared to fade into the sky. No large, natural water source supplied the area, and the creeks that cut the county could run bone dry in droughts or overflow their banks during the occasional flood. The quest to secure an adequate source of water became a persistent feature of Abilene's history. Other problems, such as gunfights in the streets, were short-lived. Abilene pioneers worked together to make their prairie town, dubbed the "Queen City," an attractive place to live. By the turn of the century, Abilene had begun to develop its identity.

The tent city hastily created before the lot sale soon evolved into a bustling community with businesses that catered to the ranching industry and to a growing populace. Townspeople moved from their tents or dugouts (homes of mud dug into the earth) by the railroad tracks into simple wood-framed cottages along the newly plotted residential streets. Churches, schools, and businesses represented the energy and virtues the community wanted to promote. But, saloons, gambling establishments, and houses of ill repute prospered, threatening the wholesome quality that Abilene visionaries hoped to achieve.

One of the early voices in promoting the values of a family community was the town's newspaper, *The Abilene Reporter*. Editor Charles E. Gilbert printed his first edition in a tent on June 17, 1881. The operation soon moved into permanent quarters and changed from a weekly to a daily publication; on occasion, when money was tight, it reverted to weekly publication.

When a large fire swept through Abilene in August 1881, Gilbert encouraged citizens to rebuild. The editor had a personal interest in rebuilding, as the fire destroyed all of his printing equipment. The fire started in the T. S. Horn Saloon on South 1st, and, although the bucket brigade hurried to help when volunteers heard the pistol alarm, flames soon ignited an entire block of wood framed buildings. Gilbert hopped a train after he surveyed the destruction and rode to Baird, where he borrowed equipment to produce his "Extra Edition."

He estimated damages at more than $20,000, but predicted that Abilene would "Phoenix-like, rise from the ashes a finer city." The town responded to the challenge to rebuild, and Gilbert's influence through his newspaper continued unchallenged until 1883, when a fierce editorial competition developed with his rival, William Gibbs of the *Magnetic Quill*.

Gilbert and Gibbs fought for readership and its accompanying financial support; they appealed to different audiences and became embroiled in a press battle when each took opposing sides in the range wars of the 1880s. Throughout the prairie lands of the western United States, the open range cattlemen detested the new barbed-wire fences. Ranchers wanted their herds to have the freedom to roam the country for water. Supporters of the fence-building efforts believed that progress depended on enclosing and developing the frontier. Gilbert insisted that for Abilene to have any chance for growth, fence-building was an absolute necessity, and Gibbs supported the "free grass" cattle ranchers. The two editors continued viciously to attack each other in their editorials. Finally, a commentary written by Gibbs on labor unions angered Gilbert so much that the written word could no longer express his fury.

In early 1885, Gilbert took the fight out of the pressroom in what the *Taylor County News* termed, "an editorial encounter in which they [tried] to prove that the sword is mightier than the pen." Both men brought their weapons to the street, where they faced off in front of the First National Bank building and fired about five shots. After the smoke cleared, both men still stood, but a bullet had grazed Gilbert's forehead and Gibbs had somehow received a bruised arm from a whip. Both men were arrested but released shortly thereafter. The streetfight and ongoing virulent editorials almost ruined the *Reporter*, but Gilbert weathered the storm, and the newspaper he founded would become the oldest continuous enterprise in Abilene. The *Magnetic Quill* published its last edition in September 1885.

In 1883, Abilenians held two elections that eroded neighboring Buffalo Gap's influence on the surrounding area. The first election, held in January, resulted in both Abilene's incorporation and the hiring of a town marshal. The second election, held in October, wrested the Taylor County seat from Buffalo Gap. From the days of the town lot sale, Buffalo Gap had governed Abilene, but, by late 1882, the citizens of Abilene wanted control of their own affairs. The incorporation vote reflected the controversy over the range war. One hundred and four

Above: Abilene's town band posed in a wagon to advertise Wooten's Wholesale Grocers. This photo, taken around 1885, shows the Palace Hotel in the background.

COURTESY ABILENE PHOTOGRAPH COLLECTION, HARDIN-SIMMONS UNIVERSITY.

Left: The Palace, c. 1885. Abilene's first brick hotel, The Palace offered twenty-five rooms to let and was called the "Popular One Dollar House."

COURTESY ABILENE PHOTOGRAPH COLLECTION, HARDIN-SIMMONS UNIVERSITY.

fence-builders voted for incorporation while seventy-five free-grassers voted against it. The January ballot also gave Abilenians the opportunity to ensure the town's security in response to the growing number of gunfights. They elected Thomas Hill to a twofold-position as town marshal and tax collector. Incorporation moved the town toward stability but caused some hard feelings among the townsfolk.

If incorporation left some hard feelings, the fall balloting for the Taylor County seat made serious enemies in the neighboring community. In October 1883, Abilenians decided that, since they had done such a fine job of establishing their town government, they should also relieve Buffalo Gap of its burden of county government. Losing first the railroad then the administrative control of Abilene angered Buffalo Gap residents; they did not intend to relinquish anything else to the upstart town without a fight. The entire county endured fierce campaigning between the two communities before the vote as local newspapers advanced their views and as leadership in each town engaged speakers to promote their community. Apparently, Abilenians believed that neither the written word nor great orations were enough to persuade Taylor County residents to vote for Abilene, because the Abilene town band traveled around the county performing free concerts. Perhaps more important, the band offered free "Vote for Abilene" whiskey to listeners. Rural Taylor County residents may have enjoyed the whiskey, but they ultimately cast their votes for Buffalo Gap. When the ballots were tallied, however, Abilene overwhelmingly won the

election 905 to 269. Buffalo Gap residents cried fraud, leveling accusations that Abilenians bought votes and imported non-residents into town on trains the day of the election.

The ordeal intensified when Buffalo Gap court officials refused to surrender the county archives to Abilene. County commissioners agreed to meet in Buffalo Gap to decide the issue. On the day the judges were to hear the case, an armed group from Abilene rode to Buffalo Gap, ready to defend their perceived rights with bullets. As the Abilenians approached the rival community, they received word that their Buffalo Gap counterparts were waiting with guns loaded. The Abilene posse finally waved the white flag and both sides laid down their weapons. Five judges heard the case and verified the election returns by a vote of three to two in favor of Abilene. Some disgruntled men attempted to intimidate the judge who cast the tie-breaking vote. On the evening after the vote, they went to the judge's house to confront him. Not finding the judge at home, they killed his chickens in revenge.

Despite the commissioners' ruling, Buffalo Gap refused to deliver the records. Governor John Ireland now entered the fray, ordering the

old county seat to turn over the documents. Buffalo Gap still refused. According to Abilene historian Juanita Zachry, several stories concerning the final recovery of the court records

Above: The Taylor County Jail, built in Abilene in 1895, was located behind the county courthouse; it was razed in the 1930s.
COURTESY ABILENE PRESERVATION LEAGUE.

Left: Wagons laden with cotton travel north on Pine Street to North 3rd in front of the new Federal Building, c. 1900.
COURTESY ABILENE PHOTOGRAPH COLLECTION, HARDIN-SIMMONS UNIVERSITY.

Above: This view of Pine Street looking north, c. 1885, reveals the diversity of Abilene businesses. A bank, drug store, land agent, saddlery, and saloon are easily identified. The Cattle Exchange Saloon on the far right edge of the photo was the site for at least one of the town's deadly gunfights.
COURTESY ABILENE PHOTOGRAPH COLLECTION, HARDIN-SIMMONS UNIVERSITY.

Right: Early fires were devastating because the whole town was constructed with lumber. Fire fighting was limited to the speed with which the bucket brigade could refill and pass containers of water. As the town modernized, volunteer firemen used horse-drawn pump wagons with hoses to extinguish flames. This photo was taken circa 1892.
COURTESY ABILENE PHOTOGRAPH COLLECTION, HARDIN-SIMMONS UNIVERSITY.

circulated: Sheriff Kinch V. Northington hired a crew to retrieve them; District Judge T. B. Wheeler seized the records, loaded them into his buggy, and brought them to their new home in Abilene; or Commissioner F. I. Murray moved the documents in saddlebags. No matter what the method, by November 1883, the records had been peacefully transferred to Abilene. This exciting affair concluded without bloodshed, but other local disputes were often more violent.

Gunfights in Abilene regularly occurred in close proximity to saloons—apparently everything in early Abilene happened close to a saloon. In January 1884, one particular argument in the Cattle Exchange Saloon on Pine Street turned violent. After a burst of about twenty shots, a gambling house owner, a deputy marshal, and the marshal's brother lay on the floor of the saloon, two of them dead, one mortally wounded. The town continued to experience deadly gunfights at such an alarming rate that, according

to Abilene Police historian David Fuller, the town's second marshal, W. A. George, found the job too dangerous and quit. Deputy John J. Clinton stepped in to fill the unexpired term and met with great success over his long tenure.

The citizens of Abilene appreciated Clinton's firm hand with rowdy saloon patrons and elected him to his own term as marshal in 1888. Clinton was no newcomer to the area. He arrived in Abilene in the mid-1880s and quickly helped the community achieve a sense of law and order (he also served as assistant fire chief). Abilenians responded to his genuine concern for the well-being of the community and elected Clinton to the position of fire chief in 1889. He continued in this dual role until his death in 1922.

Clinton developed a reputation as a man who would not tolerate nonsense. One of the more visible signs of his commitment to law and order occurred every New Year's Eve. From his early days as a deputy to the end of his life, Clinton stood on the corner of South 1st and Chestnut to see out the old year. At midnight, he fired his gun in the air as a signal for the saloons to close, and as an action designed to discourage disorderly behavior. Abilene continued to witness occasional deadly outbursts, but promotional materials produced by the newspapers downplayed any negatives and indicated that Abilene was a wonderful place to live.

In April 1884, the *Magnetic Quill* published a Trade Guide and City Directory, a lengthy bulletin that described the "enterprising county seat" and listed local businesses and residents. This brochure informed locals about their community and invited potential businesses to the area. William Gibbs touted Abilene as the "Queen City on the picturesque prairie of the world" and noted that natural resources included fertile soil and flowing streams of "fine water." The community, he maintained, boasted "intelligent, law-abiding citizens," who supported three basic pillars of economic and social stability: businesses, churches, and schools.

Business represented the first pillar of stability, and Abilene featured every trade necessary for making a proper town. The community developed into a horse and cattle shipping center and possessed the second-largest wool market in Texas. Businesses included banks, drug stores, retail stores, and hotels. Doctors, den-

❖

Marshal John J. Clinton, c. 1900.
Clinton was reported to have served
as a marshal in Dodge City, Kansas
prior to his move to Abilene.
COURTESY ABILENE REPORTER NEWS.

tists, and attorneys opened offices near downtown, and women owned and operated millenaries and boarding houses. Advertisements reflected the merchants' confidence for Abilene's future. With the town government firmly established, the first mayor, B. D. Corley (1883-1885), worked with five town aldermen to administer the community's growth.

Gibbs estimated Abilene's 1884 population at 2,500. While the majority of the population was white, there were a few minorities, about "150 negroes and Chinese [and] a few Mexicans" who called Abilene home, but Gibbs indicated that it was difficult to obtain an exact count, as they "constantly" moved from one house to another. An earlier promotional brochure placed the average age of local businessmen at thirty-five,

Top, left: Model Laundry, located at North 3rd and Mesquite, c. 1890.

Top, right: The Presbyterian Church soon moved from a tent to a clapboard building that housed the school. In 1884, a building campaign began, and the church was dedicated in 1885. The tracks in front of the building indicate that the photo was taken after the turn of the century, approximately 1910.

Bottom: The town grew considerably in its first twenty years, brick structures replaced clapboard buildings, and the town boundaries expanded with the addition of Simmons College. This bird's eye view looks north, c. 1900.

with entrepreneurs moving to Abilene from all over the country as well as Europe. This positive commercial environment stabilized the town's economy, while residents focused on religion and education as the bulwarks for their move toward a more virtuous and refined society.

This second pillar of stability, churches, established the moral tone for the community. Religious revival was on the rise in late nineteenth-century America, and the new frontier town fully embraced this missionary fervor. Presbyterians raised their tent church in February 1881, but as increasing numbers of evangelists and missionaries made their way to the "Queen City," tents gave way to more enduring structures. By late fall 1884, Methodists boasted two buildings, Baptists occupied a church on the corner of North 4th and Cedar, and Episcopalians worshipped in a small stone building. Disciples of Christ and Presbyterians continued to meet in homes or temporary facilities, but each had begun building campaigns. In 1885, the Mt. Zion Baptist Church welcomed

African-American worshippers; this church family would be instrumental in developing education for blacks in Abilene. At the turn of the century new churches, representing Catholics, Lutherans, and Christian Scientists took form. The Abilene Church of Christ organized in 1903, and a Jewish synagogue opened during the 1940s.

Early residents identified education as the third pillar of stability for Abilene. Citizens called the first town meeting to organize a school. Like many businesses and churches, the first classes met in a tent in 1881. After Abilene incorporated in 1883, the town took control of the schools; students studied mathematics, English, physics, Latin, and geography. As the town grew and the school-age population increased, school officials arranged for classes to meet in a series of temporary facilities.

In 1887 about 364 students met in a rented warehouse nicknamed the "Beer and Ice Seminary" (beer and ice had been stored there previously). The following year, six young people comprised the first graduation class from an Abilene school. In 1889, townspeople pooled their resources to construct a new high school near the corner of South 1st and Peach Streets. Around 1890 a school for black students opened with twenty-two children attending. By 1900, Abilene's school system included the high school, two schools for white children (one on the north side of town and one on the south side), and one school for black children. About 800 students attended the Abilene schools. Even as the community sought to meet the educational needs of their younger citizens, leaders recognized the value, both economically and morally, of higher education.

In 1890, a group of Abilenians led by Henry Sayles and K. K. Legett lobbied the Baptist Association for an institution of higher learning. The men anticipated Abilene's growing regional importance and hoped that a college or university might stimulate Abilene's development. A religious institution fit well with the goals of the upright community. Abilene businessmen worked with church leaders to secure pledges of $5,000 to construct a school. They also located acreage suitable for a campus about two miles north of the railroad depot. As local boosters promoted what became known as Abilene Baptist College, a New York preacher and phi-

lanthropist named James B. Simmons was impressed by the efforts to provide Christian education. He donated more than $12,000 to the new school that began classes in September 1892. Upon his death, Simmons left the college his estate, and its name was changed to Simmons College in 1900.

In the 1890s, other signs suggested that Abilene was developing a more refined vision for the community. The population had grown to 3,194, and, along with business, religious, and educational goals, the town began to

Above: Abilene's first permanent public school opened in January 1890. It was located on the corners of North 1st and Peach Streets. The building was torn down in 1924.
COURTESY ABILENE PHOTOGRAPH COLLECTION, HARDIN-SIMMONS UNIVERSITY.

Left: Lytle Lake, c. 1909. Abilene thought that Lytle Lake would solve the town's water problem. The water supply gave Abilene an edge in securing state funding for an epileptic hospital in 1901, but droughts in the early decades of the new century sent the town looking for additional sources.
COURTESY ABILENE PHOTOGRAPH COLLECTION, HARDIN-SIMMONS UNIVERSITY.

emphasize cultural endeavors. Electricity drew Abilenians downtown to enjoy attractions in the evenings, and two opera houses anchored the entertainment center. Citizens also joined social clubs that encouraged positive, moral activities in the community; the Reading Club (renamed the Shakespeare Club) and the Cactus Chautauqua Circle (later the XXI Club) attracted the town's elite women. The community band performed concerts in Abilene and neighboring towns and, although their lively music provided an acceptable form of entertainment, dancing to the music did not. Preachers across Abilene united to oppose the evils of dancing. Sermons admonished parishioners to avoid both this lewd activity and the accompanying seduction of alcohol.

Temperance advocates lectured across the United States in the late nineteenth century, and Abilenians promptly responded to the message, adding their voices to those of the national reformers. As the town continued to market its increasingly moral community to settlers, they determined that a restriction on the sale and consumption of alcohol might provide the needed inducement for families to locate in Abilene. In the Texas referendum of 1887, Abilene and Taylor County voted for prohibition, but alcohol remained legal throughout the state. In 1894, locals called for a countywide election that resulted in a loss for temperance activists; Taylor County remained wet. Nonetheless, the teetotalers triumphed in a 1902 election. The last legal sale of alcohol in Abilene occurred in 1903. Although the liquor question continually resurfaced, alcohol would not legally be sold again for three-quarters of a century.

Another issue that regularly plagued Abilene was also a wet/dry problem, but it involved the constant struggle to secure and maintain a permanent water source. Early efforts to provide water for the town proved largely inadequate. Abilenians relied on water from Lytle and Cedar Creeks, and, if a resident could not fetch the water, water-haulers would deliver it at a cost of twenty-five cents per barrel. Most Abilenians kept a barrel just outside their home for daily use, but haulers delivered only every other day. Since there was no water filtration, it simply sat in the barrel until it was needed. In the heat of summer, the tepid water inevitably invited disaster. Typhoid and other infectious diseases became such a serious problem toward the end of the century that "pest houses" were set up away from the residential areas to care for the sick.

Abilene attempted a number of options to acquire a water source closer to town. Officials had sunk wells in town only to discover salt water. They used a pipeline from the creeks, but it did not provide enough water. Finally, the town tried a standpipe collection system but it, too, failed to offer a suitable solution. Long dry spells exacerbated existing water problems; by the late 1880s the situation appeared desperate.

A drought, which began during the relentless winter of 1885-86, extended through most of 1887. During a twenty-three month period, only trace amounts of rain fell. The parched land offered little water for the town and provided even less for livestock (the open-range cattle industry would reorganize after this terrible experience). The entire county became so dry that American Red Cross representative Clara Barton traveled to the area to inspect the devastation. The Red Cross did not bring Abilene any relief, but other groups, including the City of St. Louis, Missouri, showed compassion through gifts of staples, sent by train, to share with the stricken community. A permanent water source for the community had now become vital.

Private enterprise came to the town's rescue in 1897. The Lytle Water Company began construction of a dam that created Lytle Lake. At the same time the water company built the dam, it laid pipe into Abilene, giving citizens a direct source. In a stroke of good fortune, the skies opened up as the dam was completed, filling the 400 million gallon lake. The company successfully pumped water into the town, ending the water problem for the time being. In 1898, the Lytle Water Company began operation of the town's electric plant and changed its name to the Abilene Power and Light Company. Abilene's modernization was underway.

Abilene's frontier mentality began to fade as the nineteenth century ended. With no geographical features to entice settlers to the area, the town relied on its citizenry to provide the attraction. To this end, they laid the cornerstones that

would support Abilene's future development. The young community quickly became a thriving commercial center that advanced sincere commitments to education and moral character. With this new emphasis on growth potential, Abilenians sought out institutions, such as Simmons College, in the belief that they would enhance the established environment and help promote standards the town counted as virtuous. As Abilenians anticipated the excitement of the new century, they looked with pride at the growing stability of a community created on the vast prairie lands by the railroad at Milepost 407.

Above: Hughes Hardware.
COURTESY ABILENE PHOTOGRAPH COLLECTION, HARDIN-SIMMONS UNIVERSITY.

Below: Area farmers suffered greatly during the droughts. Water problems plagued Abilene throughout the nineteenth and twentieth centuries.
COURTESY ABILENE PHOTOGRAPH COLLECTION, HARDIN-SIMMONS UNIVERSITY.

"A Straight-Laced Community"

The twentieth century opened full of promise for Abilene. While Abilenians prepared to leave the frontier behind, they remained committed to nineteenth century ideals of education, morality, and a stable economic base. From 1900 to 1940, Abilene welcomed changes brought by the modernization that swept the nation. Accompanying tensions, however, tempered enthusiasm during this transitional period, and the community banded together to fight perceived ills. Concerned citizens and city officials tightened controls in an effort to preserve the established moral climate. When Paramount Theater Manager Wally Akin described Abilene in 1934 as "straight-laced," the community surely felt vindicated. Even as Akin made this observation, Abilene suffered the impact of the Great Depression. Community leaders turned their energies from maintaining a pious town to locating sources that could help Abilene survive the devastation. Abilene's early twentieth-century experience was one of adjustment to progress and the strife it imposed.

Progress for Stability

Abilene kept pace with the national transformation of the new century. Beginning in 1911, a progressive, commissioner-based government controlled the city; automobiles replaced horses, dirt streets gave way to paved roads, and new technology eased everyday burdens. When range wars and water problems killed Clabe Merchant's dream of a cattle railhead, Abilenians refocused booster efforts to maintain population and economic growth. Attracting newcomers became a crusade.

As early as 1883, Charles Gilbert took an active role in promoting the town through "immigrant" newspapers that he published and mailed east. Gilbert's descriptions of Abilene promised a "prosperous future" for those willing to come to the new Texas town. As the community grew, booster organizations developed, including the West Texas Immigration Association, the Abilene Board of Trade, and Abilene's Progressive Committee. Throughout the latter part of the nineteenth century, these groups printed broadsides or held fairs to advertise Abilene to immigrants. Promotional materials targeted farmers after the turn of the century. Pictorial magazines allowed prospective settlers to see the town's development and to read encouraging excerpts from residents. While Abilenians clearly believed in their community, its growth had not met their expectations.

The 1900 census was only the second official count for Abilene, and leaders assumed that there had been substantial growth in the years since 1890. Disappointment and disbelief enveloped the community when word filtered back to Abilene that the government had recorded 3,411 residents, an increase of only 217 in ten years. In 1905, the Abilene Board of Trade conducted their own count and found that 5,000 residents, including 368 African-Americans and 149 Hispanics, lived in town. Within the year, the board of trade, committed to raising Abilene's visibility and encouraging settlement, adopted a new name—the 25,000 Club.

Their lofty goals gave rise to their name. They hoped to double the population to 10,000 by 1908 and, following that success, to reach a population of 25,000 by 1910. Despite their concentrated effort, the town again endured disappointment when the official 1910 tally recorded only 9,204 residents. Positive that they had been short-changed, the town undertook its own census. Although they located 12,000 Abilenians, both the official and unofficial counts fell well short of the goal.

In 1912, the Chamber of Commerce of the United States was founded, and Abilene's 25,000 Club responded to the national association, changing its name to the Abilene Chamber of Commerce. The chamber operated successfully for about a year, until interest waned as a similar organization, the Young Men's Booster Club, vied for membership. The two consolidated into the Abilene Chamber of Commerce in 1914. During the next twenty-five years, the chamber took on a more professional quality and evolved into the community's primary mechanism for securing growth.

In the first two decades of the twentieth century, Abilene's industrial and business communities kept up with the most recent technology. Abilene's gins and mills supported agricultural industries,

The nursing staff at the Abilene Epileptic Asylum found time to enjoy the moment in this photograph from 1912.

while electrical plants, water works, and natural gas companies provided homes and businesses with the newest and most convenient utilities. Improvements in the telephone system made it easier for Abilenians to communicate with each other. Two telephone companies had offered service in the late 1890s, but early subscribers could not talk to their neighbors unless both used the same company. After the turn of the century, the telephone system expanded and became more accessible, so that, by 1913, more than 1,000 Abilenians enjoyed this communication sensation. While technological advances made life easier for residents, new and improved forms of transportation expanded fiscal and physical boundaries.

Local businessman William G. Swenson played an important role in helping Abilene to update and improve local and long-distance transportation. Swenson was one of the first Abilenians to experiment with the vehicle that would replace the horse and buggy—the automobile. One of Swenson's fellow open-minded Abilenians, John Guitar, purchased the town's first car, a Thomas Flyer, in 1903, even as the industry was in its infancy. Guitar became disenchanted with the vehicle, and within a few short weeks he sold it to Swenson.

The automobile and the convenience it offered captivated Abilene. The city paved streets, while new businesses, including motor companies and garages, supported the growing industry. Swenson enjoyed the convenience of the automobile, but he recognized that another railroad offered a more important reward for the town.

Since the Texas and Pacific Railway provided service for east-west connections, Abilenians hoped to capitalize on their railroad heritage by bringing a north-south line through town. Abilene lobbied railroad companies for short-lines but lost out to Cisco and Buffalo Gap. When the community decided to build its own line in 1906, Swenson organized the Abilene and Southern Railway Company. He worked closely with Colonel Morgan Jones, who in the late nineteenth century had been instrumental in meeting a tight deadline for building the Texas and Pacific line into Fort Worth. Jones currently

❖

Above The 25,000 Club Band, c.
1907. The 25,000 Club evolved into
the Abilene Chamber of Commerce.

Left: The fire department modernized
in the early part of the century to
"keep pace with the march of
progress." Fire engines and trucks,
shown in this photograph from 1926,
replaced outdated horses and wagons.
The new motorized vehicles cut
response time, and newer equipment
made the firefighters' jobs easier.

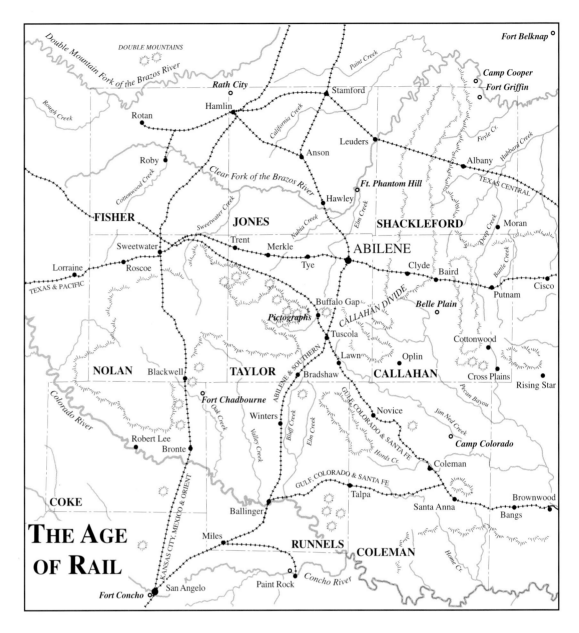

THE AGE OF RAIL

owned a railroad in Colorado and wanted to improve connections from Texas. He built the line from Abilene north to Wichita Falls, and, in 1908, extended tracks south toward Ballinger with the Abilene and Southern. While Abilene welcomed the increased rail traffic and accompanying profits, local residents were more enthused by Swenson's cross-town trolley.

Swenson contributed to Abilene's early development in several ways. He ran the Abilene Light, Water and Ice Companies, which evolved into the West Texas Utilities Company in 1923, and helped Abilene grow beyond its boundaries when he founded a new housing addition, "College Heights," on the outskirts of town near Simmons College. At the same time, Swenson served as president of the Abilene Street Railway Company, organized to operate an electric trolley system. The trolley connected the far limits of town, from Simmons College on the north to the new Alta Vista area southwest of town. When the tracks were completed in the early winter of 1908, the railway company arranged a trial run of a trolley car, dubbed the *Galloping Goose*. The short journey was supposed to give townsfolk a glimpse of the future, but the ride's climactic end resulted in more excitement than organizers had anticipated.

On Sunday afternoon, November 29, 1908, community leaders boarded the *Galloping Goose* for the ride south. Swenson served as conductor and brakeman for the trolley's jaunt through undeveloped sections of town. As passengers enjoyed a pleasant, uneventful trek the trolley picked up considerable speed toward the end of the line. Swenson forcefully applied the brake but had no luck slowing the pace. He sounded the whistle as the trolley exploded through the end of the tracks. Momentum propelled the trolley forward, and, as it "smashed [a pole] to kindling," riders standing on the trolley's platform were tossed helter-skelter into a muddy field. The trolley pitched forward into a mud pit, where it remained stuck for sever-

al hours. Once by-standers realized that no one was seriously injured, they enjoyed a good laugh. This event notwithstanding, Abilene's improved transportation enterprises helped the town establish a regional presence and promoted the local business and professional community.

With growing professionalism in the dental and medical fields, Abilene became a regional medical center, supported by both public and private funding during the early years of the new century. Abilene secured financial support from the Texas Legislature in 1901 for a state care facility, the Abilene Epileptic Asylum. The institution officially opened in 1904. In 1957, the asylum

Above: The town's generating station photographed in 1923, when the power company took the name West Texas Utilities. WTU owned and operated several other businesses, gradually giving them up to concentrate on electricity. Its streetcar and bus service operated until 1931, its gas business closed in 1941, and WTU phased out their water and ice businesses in the 1950s.
COURTESY ABILENE PHOTOGRAPH COLLECTION, HARDIN-SIMMONS UNIVERSITY.

Left: Abilene's first public transit system was an electric trolley operated by Abilene Street Railway Company. Douglas Floyd and Ray Ward pose with what is likely the infamous ""Galloping Goose," c. 1908.
COURTESY ABILENE PHOTOGRAPH COLLECTION, HARDIN-SIMMONS UNIVERSITY.

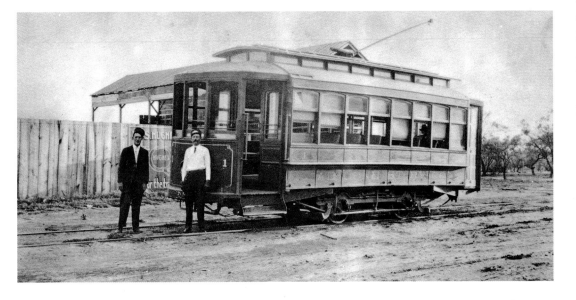

Above: The new epileptic colony grounds boasted groomed lawns and a farm with livestock. The administration building is shown here, c. 1910.

COURTESY GRACE MUSEUM.

Below: Former President Theodore Roosevelt stumped his way through the South in 1911, seeking the presidency again on the Progressive Party ticket. Roosevelt might not have intended to speak in Abilene, but an enthusiastic crowd of 4,000 compelled his train to stop. Roosevelt thrilled the crowd when he recalled his friend Hashknife Simpson and praised Abilene's schools. The Grace Hotel shows in the background. It was constructed in 1909; the depot was completed in 1910.

COURTESY ABILENE PHOTOGRAPH COLLECTION, HARDIN-SIMMONS UNIVERSITY

changed its name to the Abilene State School and focused on long-term care for mentally handicapped patients. The State School became a vital component of the community.

Two privately funded hospitals, Alexander Sanitarium, located on North 6th, and Hollis Sanitarium, on the southern outskirts of town, opened in 1904. These sanitariums offered the only hospital services between Fort Worth and El Paso. The Alexander Sanitarium was converted to a nurses' training school in 1918 and closed in 1934; the Hollis Sanitarium served patients until the early 1920s. About the time Hollis Sanitarium closed, Simmons College trustees voted to support a new facility. After receiving support from the local Baptist community, West Texas Baptist Sanitarium, later Hendrick Memorial Hospital, opened its five-story building in 1924. While new medical institutions improved healthcare in the area, Abilene's continued commitment to Christian education resulted in the addition of two new colleges.

In 1906, the Abilene Church of Christ, which had been meeting since 1903, accepted responsibility for a new school. Colonel J. W. Childers sold school trustees 5.5 acres and a house for a primary, secondary, and junior college Bible school. Childers Classical Institute, located on North 1st Street, held its first classes in the fall of 1906. Soon the *Reporter* referred to the new school as the "Christian College." In 1919, the school's status changed to a senior college, and in 1920 trustees adopted the name Abilene Christian College (ACC). The institution emerged as an essential element of the community. In the mid-1920s, when trustees decided to move the school, the city of Abilene promised financial support for relocation costs in return for ACC's promise to remain in Abilene. ACC located land that had been part of the old Hashknife Ranch and moved to the new campus in 1929. The city had practiced non-denominational support for its colleges, and when a chance arose in the early twenties to establish a Methodist college, Abilene stood firmly behind it.

Abilene enjoyed the status brought by church-supported colleges and tried to bring a state college to town prior to World War I. Although Abilenians enthusiastically promoted their town to state officials, Lubbock received the new institution. The disappointment, however, was short-lived. In the early 1920s, Methodist minister J. W. Hunt contacted city officials about the possibility of locating a Methodist college in Abilene. While some Abilenians thought three church-related schools might be too many for the town, leadership recognized the importance of the association. The city indicated that if the school agreed to

locate in Abilene, they would guarantee land, cash, and water rights, and would extend trolley lines to the proposed location just south of town. McMurry College, named for Bishop William Fletcher McMurry, presiding bishop of the Northwest Texas Conference, opened as a junior college in 1923. The college received accreditation as a senior college in 1925. That same year Simmons College amended its constitution and changed its name to Simmons University. In 1930, the chamber boasted that Abilene's church-related schools, combined with the public school system, made the city the "Athens of the West."

During the years before World War II, Abilene's public school system expanded to keep pace with a steadily increasing student population. But, until the introduction of New Deal programs in the 1930s, new AISD construction benefited only Abilene's white students. Two new elementary schools were built in 1902, and a new high school, located at South 3rd and Peach, opened in 1909. Demand for

Above: Members of Mt. Zion Baptist Church posed outside the church building, c. 1920. Church members encouraged black education when they offered their church building as a temporary school for the children at the turn of the century.

COURTESY GRACE MUSEUM.

Below: A crowd gathered in 1911 to watch as the Wooten Wholesale Grocers burned to the ground. H. O. Wooten established his wholesale company in 1898. He also built the Paramount Theater and the Wooten Hotel in the 1930s.

COURTESY ABILENE PHOTOGRAPH COLLECTION, HARDIN-SIMMONS UNIVERSITY.

more space resulted in the addition of a larger high school, at South 1st and Peach, in 1923. The older southside building converted to an elementary school. When construction of another elementary school was completed in 1922 in the College Heights area, white students vacated the older building, which was retained for use by black students.

At the turn of the century, the Abilene Colored School housed all grades together in a one room clapboard building. In 1902, crowded conditions led the Mt. Zion Baptist Church to invite the school to meet at their location until arrangements could be made for a larger structure. Abilene's African-American population decreased between 1910 and 1920 (from 602 to 410), but

by 1930 census records indicated the number had increased to 1,403. Although school attendance mirrored the general growth of Abilene's black community, the school system held the number of teaching positions at the black schools to two—in 1921, a two teacher, one room facility served eighty-four students. The vacated College Heights building housed the "Colored School" from 1922 until 1936, when a new campus with a ten room building opened on North 9th Street, courtesy of New Deal funding.

While the public school system benefited the majority of the population, private education appealed to a select few. In 1900, the Cooper Training School for Boys opened, but financial problems forced it to close in 1914. The buildings of the school were taken over by the Catholic Church, and the Sisters of Divine Providence opened St. Joseph's Academy in 1916. Childers Classical Institute opened in 1906 with elementary and secondary components. Abilene's commitment to education received a boost in 1909 with the opening of the Carnegie Library. Education continued to provide a pivotal base for the community, but Abilenians also found time to enjoy new leisure activities that swept the nation.

Hollywood came to Abilene in 1912, when the first theater, the Royal, opened. Silent pictures entranced Abilenians, and soon the Mission, the Queen, the Gem, the Oasis, and the American Theaters were built to accommodate

the crowds. When Hollywood introduced "talkies" in the late 1920s, audiences thronged to see and hear the newest shows at the most up-to-date theaters, including the Majestic, the Rex, and the Palace. Even while moving pictures delighted townspeople, live performances continued to captivate Abilenians.

Opera companies, theater troupes, acrobats, and orators traveled throughout the Southwest during the first decades of the century and regularly entertained Abilene audiences. Performances increased in the '20s as nationally recognized figures such as Will Rogers, former president William Howard Taft, and John Philip Sousa visited Abilene. The town also enjoyed fads that defined the twenties. Crowds looked skyward downtown and thrilled at the sight of the "human fly," Henry Roland, climbing the eight-story Mims Building in 1928. The following year Benny Fox sat on his flagpole seat on the Hilton Building for 100 hours.

One of the largest gatherings occurred when Charles Lindbergh landed his *Spirit of St. Louis* in Abilene. Lindbergh had completed his solo transatlantic flight in May 1927. Upon his return to the United States, he embarked on a nationwide tour to promote aviation. Abilene leaders were delighted with the prospect of having a national hero in the community and planned a hearty Texas welcome. They anticipated a large crowd, so the evening before "Lucky Lindy" was to arrive, local boy scouts

spent the night at the airport. On the morning of September 26, 1927, the boy scouts served as crowd control when Lindbergh flew into Abilene's Kinsolving Airport from Santa Fe, New Mexico. After a hero's welcome at the airport, Lindbergh rode at the head of a parade into town. Well-wishers greeted him as he mounted the steps at the bandstand behind the Federal Building. He spoke briefly about the future of commercial aviation, enchanting the audience with his humble demeanor. While Abilenians enjoyed these more short-lived entertainment episodes, regular events held at Abilene's Fair Park offered recurrent diversions for the town.

Abilene's first fair, held in 1883, established a precedent for the annual event, but the fair had no permanent home. Around 1910, a civic minded group decided that a developed fairgrounds

The racetrack at Fair Park hosted horse, motorcycle, and automobile races. Inside the course, football and polo players made good use of the field. Football captivated Abilenians in the 1920s, when Coach P. E. Shotwell led the Abilene High Eagles to state titles. Fair Park is now Oscar Rose Park.

COURTESY GRACE MUSEUM AND
ABILENE PHOTOGRAPH COLLECTION,
HARDIN-SIMMONS UNIVERSITY.

and city park might help promote growth. They purchased forty acres south of town, then deeded the land to the city; Fair Park was born. The city continued to sponsor the annual fair until the West Texas Fair Association organized in 1921. The association successfully boosted fair attendance, which often exceeded 40,000. The fair and park complex grew to include display buildings, a racetrack, a football field, and—sometime between 1923 and 1925—a zoo. Fair Park became the focal point for Abilenians' activities.

Abilene became an urban center in the early years of the twentieth century. New technology improved lifestyles and, although expectations of population growth fell short, town leaders worked to make Abilene a modern city. A general atmosphere of optimism overshadowed disappointment when the 1920 census reported 10,274 residents. New transportation, better medical care, an expanding educational system, and cultural development secured Abilene's position as a regional hub. By 1930, the population had more than doubled to 23,175. But progress came at a cost. Change presented challenges for the community; Abilene responded with renewed commitment to virtuous living and, in the days of the Depression, with a renewed drive to regain economic strength.

STRIFE AND INSTABILITY

Abilene welcomed the changes brought on by progress, but disruptive forces threatened to destroy the harmony of the town. The Great War (World War I) imposed the city's first major ordeal of the century, and in its aftermath, social change introduced standards contrary to established ideals. The city, in concert with churches and colleges, responded to the threat with determination. At the same time, Abilene's economy soared and the town's prosperity served to delay the onset of the Great Depression. But the national catastrophe soon hit Abilene with full force. Still, the city and the chamber actively pursued state and national funding to keep the town solvent. Abilene met challenges head-on in order to maintain the established social order and a solid economic base.

Like the rest of the country, Abilene felt the burden that came with America's entry into World War I in 1917. President Woodrow Wilson ordered the conscription of young men to augment the small numbers then serving in the regular Army and National Guard. Abilene's National Guard unit had organized in 1916, and student armies drilled on the three college campuses. In 1918, area men of Company I, Seventh Regiment, reported for active duty and trained at Fair Park, where broomsticks substituted for rifles in drills. The company became part of the 142nd Infantry, Thirty-sixth National Guard Division of Texas and completed its training at Camp Bowie in Fort Worth. Tragedy struck while at Bowie when a trench mortar exploded and killed four Abilenians. Company I shipped out to Europe in July 1918. Other Abilenians answered the call as well. In all, thirty-two local men lost their lives in service to their country during the war.

In the aftermath of the Great War, a sense of euphoria enveloped the country. This overwhelming enthusiasm quickly found its way to West Texas. Abilene's elders worried about the "deplorable condition of the youth" as teenagers experimented with new dance steps, disappeared unchaperoned in automobiles, and watched lurid scenes on the town's movie screens. Churches momentarily forgot doctrinal differences as they banded together to condemn modern dancing while the city regulated flirting and motion pictures showings.

In 1926, the chamber touted Abilene as a place where churches and schools came first. They bragged that three Bible colleges and one church for every 961 people made Abilene a "clean moral city." Educational and religious institutions strongly influenced the town's codes. Not only did laws prohibit Sunday

picture shows and ball playing, but ordinances even addressed personal conduct.

In 1925, a statute outlawed unwanted advances by "word, sign, gesture, or wink." The edict further stipulated that it was "Unlawful for any male person…to make…'goo-goo' eyes" at any woman in public. The misdemeanor was punishable by a fine of up to $200. Abilene had instituted its own prohibition in 1902, so the Eighteenth Amendment to the United States Constitution (Prohibition), which went into effect in 1920, did not influence the town significantly (even when the Eighteenth Amendment was repealed during the Depression, Abilene remained dry). Abilenians had long before devised methods to circumvent the local law; private club membership and prescription whiskey made alcohol easily accessible. In fact, Abilene's bootlegging industry caused one judge to charge there was a veritable "underworld" in the city.

The colleges supported limitations imposed by the city and endorsed by the churches. The religious institutions went a step further and added a few more restrictions of their own, including a rule at ACC that prohibited card playing. The colleges worked as partners with the churches and the city to ensure that their students respected the moral atmosphere imposed by the community. Another organization rallied during the twenties to preserve Abilene's traditional values—the Ku Klux Klan.

Abilene's Klan made its first public appearance in 1921, when the local newspaper announced the organization's $100 donation to the Salvation Army. The Klan gained membership and organized a demonstration to show their strength for Thanksgiving Eve, 1921. Newspaper articles publicized the coming parade, and on Thursday evening a large crowd lined downtown streets at dusk to watch the procession. At dark streetlights were extinguished and spectators looked on as more than 200 hooded Klansmen marched silently behind a burning cross.

While the national Klan organization targeted foreign-born Americans, it appeared that Abilene's Klan adopted the older custom of attacking local minorities. 1922 was the most violent year for Abilene's vigilantes and featured abductions, whippings, and beatings. One incident ended with the death of a black man; the murder was attributed to the Klan, but the charge went unpunished. By 1924, on both the local and national levels, Klan membership

Above: Pictured here are Dave and Earsie Brown, owners of Dave and Earsie's Restaurant. Dave and Earsie's Restaurant weathered the storm of the Depression, opening only on weekends. They welcomed the arrival addition of the Army in the 1940s, when their workdays extended often into the late nights.

COURTESY GRACE MUSEUM.

Right: The Federal Building facing North 3rd Street, off Pine, c. 1927. The Federal Lawn, the bandstand, and the Hilton Hotel are shown directly behind. The bandstand was torn down in 1936, and the Hilton Hotel became the Windsor in 1947.

COURTESY ABILENE PHOTOGRAPH COLLECTION, HARDIN-SIMMONS UNIVERSITY.

Abilene enjoyed a prosperous economy during the 1920s as the town developed into a regional hub of activity. New construction filled needs for additional hotel and office space as well as for leisure activities. Building projects of the twenties helped to delay the impact of the stock market crash of 1929 and the ensuing crisis of the Depression. In 1925, construction started on Abilene's first skyscraper, the Alexander Building. By the mid-twenties, the seven-story Hilton Hotel and the eight-story Mims Building had been added to the landscape. Two cash projects begun in 1929 by Horace O. Wooten, the Paramount Theater and the sixteen-story Wooten Hotel, opened in the early years of the Depression. While the effects of the nationwide collapse were slow in reaching Abilene, the city felt the full impact by 1932.

Plummeting agricultural and oil prices hit the Abilene area hard, and the initial response was to rely on community benevolence. The United Welfare Association, founded in 1929, was among the earliest local charities to respond to needy families. Soon, Abilene's non-profit institutions experienced severe cutbacks. When attendance at the local colleges dropped sharply, ACC and Simmons University received substantial gifts from John J. Hardin to keep their doors open; consequently, the Baptist school changed its name to Hardin-Simmons University in 1934. The Thomas Hendrick family gave financial

tapered off, and the Abilene organization disappeared in 1926. The Klan advocated protection of traditional mores, but their actions were more destructive to the community than beneficial. If social disturbances prompted the community to take a stand for morality, the Great Depression forced the city to pursue outside funding sources to keep Abilene financially sound.

assistance to the West Texas Baptist Sanitarium in 1935; the name changed to Hendrick Memorial Hospital in 1937. The Hendricks also provided funding for the Hendrick Home for Children, which opened in 1939 to provide a new home for children whose families could no longer care for them. Although local charities and private donors infused much needed cash to relieve pressure, the severity of the Depression motivated the city to take advantage of governmental funding.

In January 1932, Congress approved President Herbert Hoover's Reconstruction Finance Corporation (RFC). One of the RFC's purposes was to make emergency loans for communities to spend on public works. In October 1932, the chamber of commerce reviewed the application process for the RFC and determined that, since the community wanted to employ a work relief program (as opposed to a direct hand-out), Abilene should apply for the least amount necessary, $75,000. With funding secured from the RFC, the Abilene Federal Relief Plan was underway by November. To qualify, applicants must have been Taylor County residents for at least six months. Once accepted into the program, laborers worked eight hour days for $1.50 a day for unskilled labor and $2.50 a day for skilled labor. Work crews cleaned city parks, public and rural schools, and city streets. Other participants repaired clothing to distribute among the needy. Even as Abilene received some relief from the Hoover administration, the devastated country expressed its lack of faith in the president, elect-ing Franklin Delano Roosevelt to the nation's highest office in 1932.

When FDR took office in 1933, the nation was desperate for relief. His New Deal programs reached Abilene at a critical point. The Public Works Administration, the Federal Emergency Relief Administration, the Civil Works Administration, the Civilian Conservation Corps, the National Housing Administration, the Agricultural Adjustment Administration, and the Works Progress Administration all operated in the Taylor County area to provide much needed relief. One of the more important projects approved in 1938 was construction of a dam at Lake Fort Phantom Hill.

Abilenians thought their water problems had been solved in the late 1890s with the addition of Lytle Lake. But the dam washed away in 1913, and a drought that lasted throughout 1917 and 1918 left Lytle Lake dry.

These extreme incidents prompted officials to consider building a lake that would be controlled by the city. Lake Abilene, located on upper Elm Creek, was completed in 1921. When Lake Abilene dried out due to a drought in 1927, a $600,000 bond offering funded the construction of Lake Kirby. Even with three lakes, the city considered another project in

1931, Fort Phantom Hill Dam. Although the Depression delayed the project, the city and the chamber of commerce continued to promote the additional water source. Finally in 1938, construction on the new dam began.

The chamber also considered several options to help the city's economic recovery. In 1935, a short-lived attempt to obtain the State Hospital

for Negro Tuberculars ended when a committee recommended the project should not be pursued. In 1936, it was suggested that Abilene's "superior winter climate" would certainly attract people if only the town were advertised. The following year, the chamber unsuccessfully approached Washington officials about a Veterans Hospital.

The chamber continued to court Department of War officials in 1939 and 1940, hoping to have Abilene designated as a "sub-base" for San Antonio's Kelly Field. Although this endeavor, like the previous ones, met with little response in Washington, it did lay the groundwork for a successful campaign to obtain an army training camp. When America began World War II mobilization, chamber members remembered their experiences and recognized that they needed advocacy in the nation's capitol.

UNDERPASS AND PINE STREET, LOOKING NORTH

"VITAL TO NATIONAL DEFENSE"

Abilene experienced long-hoped-for population increases and prosperity from 1940 to 1960. Census numbers swelled by 340 percent during the twenty-year period, cresting at 90,638 in 1960. Industrial and commercial development responded to and augmented this stimulation. By the late 1950s, Abilene's economy was flourishing. The crisis of World War II supplied the city with an opportunity to step out of the Depression. The unprecedented mobilization of U. S. forces spawned a booming wartime economy, and Abilene acquired the temporary army training facility, Camp Barkeley. The tent camp was designed to train about 20,000 troops, but with America's entry into the war, the facility expanded to house upwards of 50,000 men. The influx of tens of thousands of men between the ages of eighteen and twenty-two dramatically changed the city. When the government deactivated Camp Barkeley toward the end of the war, Abilene lost a powerful economic and cultural engine. Abilene was depicted in a *Life* magazine article as another tale of boom to bust, but this proved to be an erroneous prophecy. The community moved forward relying on its early tradition of self-promotion. By the early 1950s, the city had secured a permanent military facility, Dyess Air Force Base. Indeed, Abilene's relationship with the military became vital to its own security and to national defense.

THE CAMP YEARS

"A drastic change came over Abilene." This sentiment, expressed by a former Abilene resident almost fifty years after the end of World War II, captured the essence of Abilene's wartime experience. As Abilene citizens departed for the uncertainty of war, tens of thousands of "adopted" sons and daughters passed through the city during their service to their country. Men and women descended upon Abilene from all over the United States, bringing a boon to the previously depressed economy. In addition, cultural influences from the outsiders shook the established social order, forcing Abilene to develop a balancing act in its relationship with the camp. Although citizens genuinely wished to extend hospitality to the GIs, the overwhelming presence of the soldiers challenged the prevailing mores of the community.

Throughout the late 1930s and the early 1940s, the *Abilene Reporter-News* followed the advancing European war on a daily basis. As Abilenians observed the war from afar, President Roosevelt realized the potential for America's involvement and he called National Guardsmen to active duty in August 1940. While local Guard units began training near their homes, the War Department located and secured large tracts of land throughout the country for training camps.

The government established most of the training facilities in the South. Abilene leaders watched with envy as nearby Brownwood prospered from a new camp located on its outskirts. In the early fall of 1940, members of a newly formed Abilene Chamber of Commerce Military Affairs Committee visited Brownwood's Camp Bowie and envisioned how a similar installation could benefit Abilene. The committee appointed a delegation to go to Washington and promote the city. The group met with Army officials, highlighting railroad access and availability of land as prime incentives for a locating a new training camp near Abilene.

When the Army expressed interest in Abilene, city leaders searched for a site suitable for Army use. Abilene officials located and secured options on 70,000 acres of farmland approximately six and a half miles southwest of the city limits. In October 1940, Abilenians received word of the Army's approval of the proposed area. But the government had two stipulations: first, only 2,000 acres were needed and second, the land had to be purchased within one week's time.

Undaunted, optimistic citizens established a campaign headquarters downtown and threw themselves into a frenzied fundraising effort. A large thermometer was erected on a prominent street corner to measure "camp fever" as donations poured in. The *Abilene Reporter-News* endorsed the venture and featured a picture of one enthusiastic citizen hoisting "his roly-poly self along a ladder…to

HQ Company, Twelfth Armored Division, Germany, c. 1945. The intensive training experience at Barkeley toughened the men of the Twelfth. They were battle tested at Herlesheim, and the "Mystery Division" spearheaded Patton's race to the Rhine. The Twelfth also liberated Nazi concentration camps in Europe. The division's Forty-fourth Tank Battalion deployed to the Pacific, where it stormed the walls of Santo Tomas to rescue prisoners inside.

paint the first reading on the huge thermometer." The thermometer soon burst and Abilene celebrated the acquisition of a training camp. The Army was on its way but the city had only a short time to prepare.

A sense of urgency enveloped Abilene and work began immediately. Census records indicate that the population in 1940 was 26,763; 19,000 troops of the Forty-fifth Infantry Division were expected to arrive in February 1941, giving Abilene less than one hundred days to prepare. The town rallied to build the camp and to make living adjustments in town to accommodate support personnel. The tarpaper and tent camp took shape as more than 6,300 laborers worked in around-the-clock shifts, putting together water and sewer lines, and erecting temporary quarters (each floored-tent housed either four enlisted men, or one officer). The

intense activity swept up the entire community. Plentiful work and high wages attracted newcomers as well. The city experienced a spontaneous growth spurt as camp workers feverishly pushed to meet the deadline.

In January 1941, the city learned that the base would be called Camp Barkeley after Private David B. Barkley of Laredo, Texas. Barkley was one of only three Texans to receive the Medal of Honor in World War I. The hero did not spell his name with the additional "e", a clerical error accounted for the discrepancy.

Capitalizing on this new role and anxious to broadcast news of the city's fortune, the chamber of commerce promoted Abilene as the "Home for the Forty-fifth" in newspapers throughout the Southwest. Closer to home, the chamber organized an official celebration to welcome the troops. In late February 1941, after months of anticipation, a huge crowd, complete with flags and bands, gathered along city streets to cheer as the 1,104 vehicle convoy thundered through town en route to Camp Barkeley. The Army had arrived.

Abilene's economy thrived as soldiers spent their free time and paychecks in town. A few soldiers explored Abilene on March 1, 1941, their first Saturday night to escape from the intense training routine. They strolled the downtown streets, visited Charlie Blanks, a nightclub, and some witnessed a shooting at Mary's Place, a "joint" just down from Charlie Blanks. Even with this unfortunate incident, the men of the Forty-fifth Division appreciated Abilene's friendly welcome. As one soldier commented, being at Barkeley was "paradise"

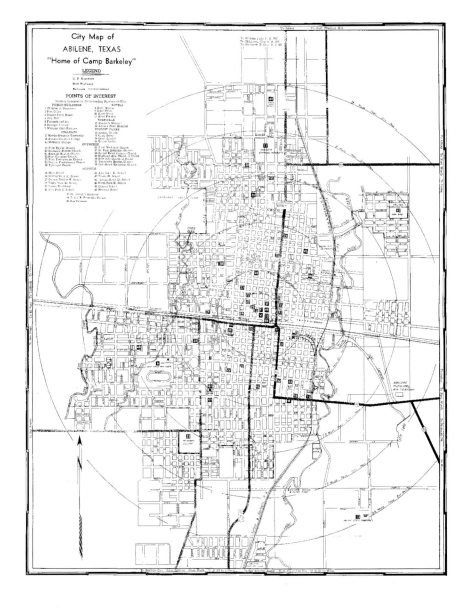

City Map of
ABILENE, TEXAS
"Home of Camp Barkeley"

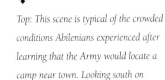

Top: This scene is typical of the crowded conditions Abilenians experienced after learning that the Army would locate a camp near town. Looking south on Chestnut Street, c. 1943.
COURTESY GRACE MUSEUM,
CAMP BARKELEY COLLECTION

Below: Calisthenics in camp proved far less demanding than the ten- to twenty-five-mile hikes that soldiers endured. The weather was often so dry that clouds of dust hovered over the camp. At other times, GIs trained in mud up to their knees.
COURTESY TWELFTH ARMORED DIVISION
MEMORIAL MUSEUM

Below: World War II gave women the opportunity to serve their country. These nurses worked at Camp Barkeley's hospital and drilled to keep in shape.
COURTESY TWELFTH ARMORED DIVISION
MEMORIAL MUSEUM

compared to Fort Sill (near Lawton, Oklahoma). Downtown streets teemed with khaki uniforms, and city leaders realized that the dearth of Abilene's diversions was going to present problems for the community.

Soldiers and locals waited in long lines for the few distractions that existed—watching movies and eating out. Matters were compounded because when the Forty-fifth arrived in Abilene, movie theaters remained closed on Sundays. As soldiers continued to stream into Abilene looking for entertainment, city commissioners recognized the difficulties posed by the ordinance; and they passed a statute that permitted theaters to open on Sunday evenings, after church. Entrepreneurs took advantage of the bustling market, opening new cafes and restaurants. But the influx of young men continued unabated, and other enterprises vied for the soldiers' attention and threatened the small-town, family atmosphere that had come to define Abilene.

Prostitution and illegal alcohol sales were the most serious issues that the community experi-

enced. The Army prodded the city to address the prostitution problem, but were puzzled by the alcohol situation. Although the city ran the prostitutes out of town (so they claimed), liquor continued to present a dilemma. Soldiers remembered long after the war that for a dry community, Abilene was soaking wet. They humorously recalled episodes of queuing up at

drugstores, obtaining twenty-five-cent prescriptions, and redeeming them for pints of whiskey. The community struggled with a desire to protect long-standing moral values and still reap the economic benefits of hosting the camp's soldiers. Abilenians understood that a transformation was underway and could potentially spiral out of control if they did not address the entertainment predicament.

The first practical solution was to provide a central meeting place for the soldiers when they came to town. Seven local businessmen purchased the 10,000-square-foot Elks Building at the corner of North 1st and Cedar, for $12,500.

Each donated $1,000 and borrowed the balance. They turned the building over to the chamber of commerce for remodeling as a soldier's recreational center. During the renovation, the city organized events to entertain the soldiers. There were free Sunday afternoon band concerts and, to help the soldiers appreciate Abilene, locals staged a "Let Us Show You Abilene" campaign. In April 1941, the newly refurbished "Recreation Hall" opened and was an immediate success.

In November 1941, the chamber negotiated with the United Service Organization (USO) to convert the Recreation Hall into a USO facility and to build a new building to house a second USO. In 1943, two more USOs opened. All four were located within walking distance of each other and the Butternut Street underpass, where Army transport dropped the soldiers. The Recreation Hall became the First Street USO and, together with the 5th Street and 2nd Street USOs, served white troops; the Mesquite Street USO opened in 1943 when black troops came to Barkeley. Volunteers at each USO provided a "home away from home" for soldiers. After long days of training, which often involved hikes of five, ten, and twenty-five miles over dusty (or muddy, depending on the year) Taylor County terrain, the USOs supplied welcome relief.

The USOs also served as a buffer between the community and the camp; they were places to

Approach to Recreation Center, Abilene State Park, Abilene, Texas

become acquainted with and share Abilene's values. Each USO developed its own character and provided many opportunities for local volunteers. Abilenians helped make the servicemen feel welcome and appreciated through myriad activities, including baking cookies, mending clothes, and even offering free legal advice from the Taylor County Bar Association. In addition, the USOs supplied books, magazines, refreshments, and stationery for the GIs. The 2nd Street USO held regularly scheduled *jam* sessions for musicians, as well as recitals and sing-alongs. Other recreational activities included badminton, shuffleboard, dominoes, checkers, and

card games; but what the youthful, energetic soldiers enjoyed most was dancing. Just as in the '20s, dancing threatened the city's virtuous reputation. So, in 1941, an all-women volunteer organization, the Bluebonnet Brigade, was formed to provide dance partners for the GIs .

The throng of young men spending free time in the community delighted young women in Abilene and the surrounding area. The women anxiously sought volunteer roles that might place them near eligible servicemen. Admission to the Bluebonnet Brigade was highly selective, and only the most suitable and preferred young women were allowed to join. The group's sponsors devised a thorough screening process and carefully chose participants who would best represent the community. The brigade's first dance was held on Halloween Eve 1941, and over the next four years more than 1,500 volunteers danced with the Barkeley boys.

Men outnumbered women by as much as ten to one at the dances; so, while the Bluebonnets danced all evening, the soldiers lined the walls around the room awaiting a loud whistle, signaling their turn to jitterbug or waltz. The Bluebonnet Brigade was only one of many volunteer efforts during the war. Abilenians sought to do their part in whatever way possible to help with the war effort, even dance.

Many Abilene families had fathers, sons, or brothers in the European or Pacific Theaters; therefore, citizens sacrificed much throughout the war to do whatever was necessary to help bring these men home. Almost every Abilenian cooperated in war-related activities, including scrap metal drives, saving fat, or planting victory gardens. Others volunteered for the Red Cross at the downtown Canteen or as Gray Ladies, who served as camp hospital volunteers. Children also found ways to participate, making cookies, serving punch, and helping with war bond drives. Rationing, too, helped to support the war. Rationing cut across socio-economic and generational lines, but Abilenians reported that the shortages did not seriously alter their lifestyles—although some women admitted to missing their stockings (the makeup they used to line the back of their legs to simulate stockings ran dripping down their legs in the West Texas summer heat).

Abilene churches rallied behind the soldiers, opening their doors to welcome them for worship on Sundays and for special activities during

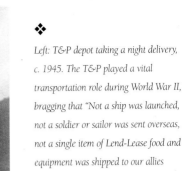

Left: T&P depot taking a night delivery, c. 1945. The T&P played a vital transportation role during World War II, bragging that "Not a ship was launched, not a soldier or sailor was sent overseas, not a single item of Lend-Lease food and equipment was shipped to our allies without first having begun the journey as raw material or finished product somewhere, sometime, on a steel rail."
COURTESY ABILENE PHOTOGRAPH COLLECTION, HARDIN-SIMMONS UNIVERSITY.

Below: Forty-fifth Infantry Division (Thunderbirds) Headquarters, c. 1942. The Forty-fifth fought with valor in Sicily, Italy, France, and Germany. Elements of the division liberated the concentration camp at Dachau in April 1945. During the war, some 3,650 men of the Forty-fifth died in combat.
COURTESY ABILENE PHOTOGRAPH COLLECTION, HARDIN-SIMMONS UNIVERSITY.

the week. With no synagogue in Abilene, a chaplain at Barkeley initiated an effort to provide a place of worship for Jewish soldiers. The camp and community cooperated to establish the Temple Mizpah in 1941.

Abilenians also opened their homes to soldiers and their wives. While most offered simple refreshment and relaxation for a few couples or servicemen, one local family hosted more than one hundred couples at a pool party, during which a magician and a strolling accordionist delighted servicemen and their wives. Abilenians labored to extend hospitality, but a housing shortage and climbing rents threatened the early relationship between town and camp.

When the city received word that the army camp was to locate near Abilene, housing construction boomed. The added population of camp building crews and the need for housing for more than 350 military families created an immediate housing shortage. New apartments sprang up, garages received quick makeovers, and residents sectioned off spare bedrooms to let to soldiers' wives. Some enterprising folks converted backyard chicken shacks into rental property. These makeshift lodgings were quickly rented, and some opportunistic residents

Above: Officer candidates keep low as they crawl through their maneuvers, c. 1942.
COURTESY TWELFTH ARMORED DIVISION MEMORIAL MUSEUM

Below: Training exercises often presented unique challenges. This photograph from 1944 shows members of the Twelfth Armored Division who ran their half track into the lake.
COURTESY TWELFTH ARMORED DIVISION MEMORIAL MUSEUM.

took advantage of the tight housing situation to raise rents.

The demand for living quarters led to an "acute" housing situation in the fall of 1941. The additional need reflected the Camp's recently expanded mission; the Medical Training Replacement Corps (MTRC) had begun training at Camp Barkeley in May 1941. The city projected that as many as 600 new housing units would be needed within a few months' time. Within a brief period the situation intensified.

America entered the war after the Japanese attacked Pearl Harbor in December 1941, and thousands of troops were expected to arrive at Barkeley during 1942. A survey of readily available rental properties revealed only twenty-five choices and, of these, only a handful were habitable; some of the properties included the chicken shacks, reportedly for rent at $9 a week. Abilene hastily initiated another building project of up to two hundred new houses, but the situation continued to deteriorate; in February 1942, the Army asked officers to leave their families behind until each could arrange for housing.

The chamber worried that the housing crisis might endanger the city's relationship with the camp, so they worked with Army officials to reach a resolution. By June 1942, some compromises

had been reached, and a Fair Rent Law was ready for approval. Camp Barkeley and Abilene experienced a significant growth spurt in the months following Pearl Harbor, and the camp's mood turned to one of urgency.

The government originally intended for Camp Barkeley to train up to 20,000 troops at any one time. As the war intensified, the camp expanded to a capacity of more than 50,000, including medical personnel trainees, Medical Administrative Corps-Officer's Candidate School (MAC-OCS), and armored battalions, as well as the original infantry component.

While the infantry and armored divisions rotated out of the camp as units at different intervals during the war, the medical training facilities underwent a constant turnover in trainees and remained active throughout the war. The MTRC trained approximately 18,000 medics

every thirteen weeks. Tens of thousands of troops cycled into the camp with their divisions or as attachments to medical units. The Ninetieth Infantry Division arrived in 1942, just before the departure of the Forty-fifth, and the officer's training school, MAC-OCS, began its operation in late 1942. At its peak operation, the camp graduated five hundred commissioned officers each week.

Camp Barkeley's training mission adapted as the needs of the war changed. In September 1943, the Eleventh Armored Division entered the gates; however, their stay at Barkeley proved short-lived as they deployed less than three months later. The Twelfth Armored Division arrived on the heels of the Eleventh and remained until August 1944. Another group called Camp Barkeley home for almost two years—as prisoners of war.

The McMurry Maidens, an all-female orchestra pictured here in December 1944, often provided musical entertainment for the Barkeley soldiers.

COURTESY JOYCE SMITH HISTORICAL COLLECTION, TWELFTH ARMORED DIVISION MEMORIAL MUSEUM.

In January 1944, the government announced the 1846th Unit Prisoner of War Camp would locate its compound at Barkeley. The 1846th accepted only German POWs and, according to one field service report, did not house any "rabid Nazi" sympathizers. Guards gave the German prisoners freedom to move about the camp and allowed them contact with civilian defense workers. POWs assisted with "housekeeping" duties, worked as mechanics, and helped with "outside work." The War Department allowed POWs the opportunity to engage in educational activities and to watch educational (propaganda) films.

POWs generally led a quiet life and did not pose any significant threats, but frightened Abilenians did not know quite what to make of highly publicized escapes. In April 1944, Abilenians read the *Reporter-News* with relief when officials recaptured two German prisoners in San Angelo. The following June, four POWs crawled through a fence in the stockade to make their break. At the peak of operation, March 1945, the prison camp housed some 820 Germans. This compound closed in April 1946, a full year after the camp's training facility deactivated.

The successful relationship between Abilene and Camp Barkeley surely influenced the Army; in June 1942, the city of Abilene received unofficial word that the government wanted to construct a large "flying field" near Tye. The Abilene

Fair Park, c. 1950. Fair Park continued to be a gathering spot for entertainment. The Round House is lit in the background.
COURTESY ABILENE PHOTOGRAPH COLLECTION, HARDIN-SIMMONS UNIVERSITY.

Army Air Field opened in September 1943, and trained airmen for P-47 "Thunderbolts." This facility housed defense workers and Army Air Corps officials for the war's duration, but the majority of those coming to the field, including 1,300 WACs, members of the Women's Army Corps, came and went.

In December 1943, the air base provided a military escort for a local funeral. The funeral was for Albany native Lieutenant Colonel William E. Dyess. Dyess had been flying in the Los Angeles area when he experienced mechanical trouble. He crash-landed, sacrificing his life to avoid killing innocent bystanders. Several airmen drove to Albany from Abilene to assist with the funeral.

After the war's end, in late 1947, the government sold the Abilene Army Air Field (sometimes called the Tye Army Airfield) to the city of Abilene for a small fee, one dollar. When Abilenians once again tried to obtain a military facility during the Cold War, the air field's track record weighed heavily in their favor. The Air Force awarded the community a new installation

that would be called, Dyess Air Force Base, after the colonel from Albany. Although the tens of thousands of soldiers from the Abilene Army Air Field and Camp Barkeley took center stage in Abilene during World War II, the community did not forget the many local men and women who served their country.

One of the first units to depart for action included local men. The Thirty-Sixth Infantry Division, Texas National Guard, reported for active duty when President Roosevelt issued the call in 1940. After training exercises at Camp Bowie in Brownwood, and after participating in a series of war games in Louisiana, the men of the Second Battalion, 131st Field Artillery, among them several Abilenians, sailed to the Pacific in the fall of 1941. The battalion proceeded to the Dutch East Indies, where in March 1942, the men were captured and spent the rest of the war in Japanese POW camps. The unit became known as the "Lost Battalion" because for more than a year there was no word of their fate.

Other Abilenians served in various branches of the armed forces stationed throughout the

PROPOSED HIGHWAY INTERCHANGE
FOR
ABILENE
LOOKING SOUTHWEST

U.S., Europe, and the Pacific. The *Abilene Reporter-News* faithfully reported on Abilene's own. The local paper kept Abilenians informed about hometown soldiers during the war years through a column called "Boys in the Service." Not only did the newspaper provide updated information on Abilene's fighting men, but it also included information useful for showing support to the troops so far from home. One reporter wrote that fruitcake was the prime gift to send abroad and included the recipe in a column so that families could bake and ship this special treat to their favorite GI. The community paid a dear and heavy price during the war—843 area men were reported killed and 3,000 were wounded.

As the war drew to a close and the need for troops waned, the War Department closed training facilities across the nation. Camp Barkeley was among of the first to close; the government deactivated the camp in April 1945, months before the official end of the war. The remaining German POWs dismantled the tent camp, and the government sold the buildings as surplus. Many of the larger structures found resting places in Abilene. Hardin-Simmons moved the Field House to the campus, and the Red Cross Headquarters relocated to North 2nd Street.

While the initial impact of the loss was significant, Abilenians had initiated a post-war strategy as early as July 1943, when the city

hired the engineering firm of Koch and Fowler to prepare a "Master City Plan." The city's leadership knew that the camp's economic boom would have to be replaced once the war was over and hoped that population gains could be extended. The loss of the camp was costly, but not unexpected.

Camp Barkeley helped Abilene grow and prosper, but the more enduring legacy was the relationship that developed between the camp and the town. The association extended beyond the time and scope of the war. Several veterans returned to Abilene to raise families, but for most soldiers, the connection was more fleeting. Still, Abilene left a lasting impression. In June 1999, at the Forty-fifth Infantry Division Historical Marker dedication, Thunderbirds reunited in Abilene after more than fifty years and recalled how the people of Abilene had made a difference as they trained for the unknown. The warm welcome they had received in Abilene gave them a sense of the people they would be fighting for.

With the advent of the Cold War, the good relations between Camp Barkeley and Abilene provided a sound foundation for the city to secure an ongoing alliance with the Pentagon. Abilenians might not have realized it at the time, but the community's future had been securely linked to the military.

❖

Abilene developed regional importance during the 1950s. This image from 1952 shows the proposed interchange for Highway 80. Highway 80 ran parallel to the T&P tracks and connected Abilene's automobile traffic to Fort Worth.

COURTESY ABILENE PHOTOGRAPH COLLECTION, HARDIN-SIMMONS UNIVERSITY.

❖

Groundbreaking for the new

air base, c. 1956.

A PERMANENT FACILITY: DYESS AIR FORCE BASE

Within one month of the Army's departure from Abilene, *Life* portrayed the city as a quiet, empty city, adjusting to the departure of the soldiers and their paychecks. The portrait testified to the radical changes Abilene experienced. Citizens could not agree about the future, one local woman observed that Abilene had become "a ghost town," while the city's newspaper editor took the military's departure in stride, forecasting that everything would be fine after a period of planning. The editor's prediction proved accurate as Abilene quickly recovered and enjoyed the attendant growth of the post-war era. A booming local economy graced the years

up to 1960. Abilene emerged as a successful regional and national oil center and through industry born of civic boosterism.

In the years following World War II, Abilene aggressively attempted to develop the town as an industrial center. A new booster organization, Abilene Incorporated, laid the groundwork to attract businesses such as Kraft, Western Cottonoil Company, Gooch Packing, and Mrs. Baird's Bakery. In 1950, the city tried to convince the United States Air Force that Abilene was a great location for a new military academy; unfortunately, the Air Force did not agree.

Industrial gains fueled population growth; by 1950 the "Key City" (the latest booster slogan)

10 Years of PROGRESS

POPULATION	LIGHT METERS	DWELLING UNITS	WATER METERS	GAS METERS
1941 28612	1941 8471	1941 8127	1941 7242	1941 7848
1951 45570	1951 16,685	1951 13,064	1951 13,678	1951 15,568

BANK CLEARINGS	BANK DEPOSITS	COLLEGE ENROLLMENTS	TELEPHONES	PUBLIC SCHOOL ENROLLMENTS
1951	1951	1941 3660	1941 7389	1941 6579
		1951 4100	1951 20,316	1951 9174

NEW AGRICULTURAL EMPLOYMENT	SQUARE MILES	BANK DEBITS	POSTAL RECEIPTS	BUILDING PERMITS
1941	1941 8.52	1941	1941	1941
1951 21,059	1951	1951	1951	1951

1941 · 1952 and still growing

87-04744.99

was home to more than 45,000 residents. Coinciding with the growth, new construction was at an all-time high with new housing, schools, commercial properties, and retail shopping centers catering to the increasingly affluent city.

The city government adapted to the post-war climate, too. In 1947, the commission form of government changed to a council-manager model. Leaders undertook projects to expand the city's limits, improve traffic safety, increase the number of fire stations, pave streets, and build bridges and parks. Abilene continued to focus on the ever-present need for a better water supply and collaborated with the Brazos River Authority on long-range plans. The city dealt not only with water and other improvements, but also with growing social ills. According to a

1955 *Abilene Reporter-News* story, the city council, concerned about the impact of violent messages on young people, passed a law making it illegal for children under eighteen to read "crime comic books."

Abilenians' continued commitment to education increased during the 1950s. The population gains benefited the public schools and, with the return of veterans, the colleges benefited from the GI Bill. The Abilene Independent School District enrollment doubled during the 1950s, and building projects barely kept up with demand during the decade. New junior high and elementary schools were built to satisfy the increasing population and three new campuses opened to high school students (Woodson High School in 1952, Abilene High School in 1955, and Cooper High School in 1960).

❖

Proud of the town's progress, the chamber of commerce threw a self-congratulatory dinner in 1952.

Although the Supreme Court had ordered desegregation during this time, Abilene's black school, Woodson, continued as a separate campus. AISD opted to integrate on a gradual basis but, by early 1963, only one school, Dyess Elementary, had integrated. The majority of Abilene's African-American students continued to attend Woodson.

Other community efforts improved Abilene's cultural and social climate, especially for the children. The city's library system expanded during the 1950s. Abilene's African-American community welcomed the addition of a library in 1953, thanks to the generosity of Eugenia Pickard, a local business woman who left her estate to benefit black education. A new Abilene Public Library building opened in 1960. A women's volunteer organization, the Junior League, focused on efforts to enhance the lives of local children, initiating a project that resulted in the founding of the West Texas Rehabilitation Center, a non-profit facility for physical therapy. The Junior League would be instrumental in future youth-oriented projects, including the Children's Museum at the Grace and the National Center for Children's Illustrated Literature. Other cultural endeavors by the community included a children's theater, and the Abilene Symphony Orchestra. Abilene's economic, social, and cultural growth did not occur in a vacuum. Abilene watched as the shadow of the Cold War spread across the country, and the city capitalized on another defense opportunity.

Abilene still owned the Abilene Army Air Field land and leaders hoped that they could turn this site to their advantage. They decided the acreage would provide the perfect location for another national defense installation. In 1950, Abilene lobbied the federal government to consider Abilene for a new military facility, but the attempt met with no response. Disappointed by the government's lack of interest, many of the same men who had worked to obtain Barkeley reunited to plan a campaign like the previous Barkeley endeavor. By 1951, the Abilene committee felt confidant of their revised approach and flew to Washington D.C. to meet with Texas representatives Omar Burleson, Tom Connally, and Lyndon Johnson, as well as with Pentagon officials.

The meetings offered encouragement, and the committee returned to Abilene with renewed enthusiasm. But, even as leaders worked to secure another military facility, America's military involvement in Korea was intensifying. The new crisis worked to Abilene's advantage. In late summer of 1951, Congress approved a substantial military budget increase and expanded the Air Force from eighty-eight to 120 wings. New bases were needed to sustain the growth.

The new post office located on Pine Street next to the Old Federal Building, c. 1958.

With Congressman Burleson's assistance, Abilene stepped up its efforts. Emissaries went back to Washington to emphasize further the advantages of the "Key City."

Shortly after the Abilenians arrived back home in September 1951, Air Force officials visited the city to assess the possibilities. The military delegates were surprised by the community's warm welcome and recommended that the community contact General Curtis E. LeMay, head of Strategic Air Command (SAC).

LeMay sent a crew to examine the area and to review the city's proposal. After their tour, LeMay's group recommended that Abilene be considered for a SAC site; the general concurred. With a favorable endorsement from the Air Force secured, Abilene waited impatiently for Congress to authorize appropriations. Abilene citizens were thrilled by the prospect of another military facility and, in an effort reminiscent of the Barkeley days, pledged nearly $900,000 to purchase additional land. The hard campaigning paid off. On July 3, 1952, Congress approved $32,273,000 for a new Air Force base to be located in Abilene.

The city celebrated the news, but at the same time officials remembered the economic disruption when Barkeley deactivated in 1945. Therefore, the city negotiated with the Air Force to build permanent structures out of concrete block rather than temporary facilities like those at Barkeley. Construction began in September 1953 on what was then called the Abilene Air Force Base; the gates opened in 1956. The name changed to Dyess Air Force Base on December 6, 1956 in honor of Albany's Colonel Dyess.

The Cold War brought the military and Abilene together again. Although Dyess has undergone organizational changes over the years, the city remains a close ally. Several awards testify to the positive relationship between Abilene and Dyess. These include the Strategic Air Command Community Support Award and the Air Combat Command Community Support Award. Abilene's bond with Dyess became a model for communities throughout the nation, and the association between the military and the community holds great promise for the twenty-first century.

A Complete City

Over the next four decades—the 1960s through the 1990s—Abilenians would find numerous opportunities to count themselves thankful for Dyess Air Force Base and the economic stability it promised. But Abilene could not rest on such promise. Memories of the bleak Depression years, an understanding of the volatile nature of agriculture and the oil business, and the realization of societal changes in America prompted city leaders to seek new ways to guarantee Abilene's future. They found the answer in diversity.

Abilene had never relied on a single cash crop or business for its survival, nor could it rely solely on the military. A diverse economy, one that accentuated traditional strengths such as education and civic development yet stood poised to exploit new opportunities, enabled Abilene to withstand formidable challenges, and indeed prosper. The last half of the twentieth century became for Abilene a time of substantial progress, fostering a powerful belief in a prosperous future. But with progress came change, and change often brought pressures that struck at the heart of Abilene's identity.

COLD WAR BASTION

The Abilene area's long association with the military, one that predated the city itself, grew even stronger after the establishment of Dyess AFB. Where dusty soldiers once guarded the Texas frontier against Comanches, men and women of the U.S. Air Force and the U.S. Army now prepared to confront threats from the other side of the world. The Cold War locked the United States in a global conflict with the Soviet Union—an anxiety-charged chess match played with intercontinental ballistic missiles, long-range strategic bombers, and massive nuclear arsenals capable of destroying the earth several times over. Abilene found itself in the middle of this struggle between titans.

Strategic Air Command brought its bombers—B-47s and later B-52s—to Dyess. These offered a mobile deterrent with which the nation could defend its interests anywhere in the world. In 1960, the region became home to a new generation of weapon, when the Air Force deployed Atlas intercontinental ballistic missiles, constructing twelve silos in six counties within a thirty-five-mile radius of Dyess. But the Altas program soon was abandoned in favor of new weapons systems. The last of the eighty-two-foot-long missiles left the Abilene area by truck in 1965; the silos were sold off for a variety of civilian uses.

Despite this formidable array of firepower, or, more precisely, because of it, Dyess and the missile sights offered a prime target, which required serious protection. To this end, in 1960, the Army established two Nike Hercules surface-to-air (SAM) missile batteries to guard the precious Air Force assets in and around Abilene. The Nike batteries stayed only slightly longer than did the Atlas program—they were deactivated in 1967.

Although the mission of Dyess AFB has changed over the years, the base remains a vital aspect of Abilene. SAC left Dyess in the 1980s, and base closure efforts, which killed Big Spring's Webb AFB among others, threatened worse still, but Dyess has survived and grown ever stronger. One important reason for this, observers say, is the unusually positive relationship between Abilene and Dyess. Such support proved instrumental when local and state leaders helped Dyess become the first base for the new B-1 bomber in 1985. The B-1 solidified Dyess' position in the ever-tightening military budget, and by the end of 1999 had demonstrated its worth with important combat deployments over Europe and the Middle East. While the B-1 remains the glamour craft of the Dyess arsenal, the sturdy C-130 remains the backbone of America's military airlift fleet. Dyess-based C-130s support military and humanitarian operations around the world and should continue to do so well into the future.

THE NOT-SO-TURBULENT '60S

The 1960s became a decade of massive social upheaval in the United States. The Civil Rights movement and the Vietnam War sparked widespread protests, urban violence, and political turmoil,

The LaJet Classic brought professional golfers, such as the popular Lee Trevino, to the new Fairway Oaks Golf and Racquet Club in 1979. Trevino's cap sports the logo of the tournament's sponsor, Abilene's LaJet, Inc.
COURTESY ABILENE REPORTER-NEWS.

but Abilene, and most of Texas for that matter, largely went about business as usual. Abilene lacked most of the provocative elements that contributed to unrest in other parts of the country. The city remained overwhelmingly white, Protestant, and conservative; it had a close and valued relationship with the military, and its citizens maintained a staunch patriotism. Change came slowly. Desegregation was achieved in the late 1960s with the closings of the proud Woodson schools. And while Abilene experienced some societal unrest, it amounted to only a fraction of the conflict that occurred in other parts of the country. But some changes, such as challenges to Abilene's prohibition on alcohol sales, proved more difficult to swallow.

Abilene's early war against local saloons and its well-cultivated reputation for wholesome living in a powerfully Christian environment were as much a part of its identity as the railroad and

the cowboy. Abilene wore its "dry" status like a badge of honor. But there had always been a bit of fiction in the word "dry," especially so after World War II. The influx of thirsty soldiers and airmen during and after the war created new demands for alcoholic beverages. Bootleggers had long prospered by selling overpriced

product to willing consumers. After the war, VFW halls could offer beer, and private clubs flourished. Members of the Abilene Country Club and the Petroleum Club could drink in high style. But for most Abilenians who desired a drink, high prices or memberships left them wanting—that is until some enterprising citizens fired the first salvo in what became a two-decade war between the "wets" and the "drys." That first shot made Impact.

IMPACT

In February 1960, a group of citizens submitted a petition to incorporate forty-seven acres in Taylor County just off the northern edge of Abilene city limits. Impact was born. Its main purpose, indeed its only real purpose, was to become an alcohol oasis in dry West Texas. But that would not happen without a fight. Church and civic leaders in Abilene attacked with fiery determination, but the quest to sell alcoholic beverages for off-premise consumption pressed

on. After a thirty-three month court battle, Impact won the right to sell package liquor, beer, and wine. Cars crammed the streets north of Abilene as Impact opened for business just days before Christmas 1962.

In 1965, residents of Buffalo Gap south of Abilene voted by a margin of one to approve on-premise sales of alcohol by restaurants in a small section of the village, making it a favored destination for many local diners. With Impact to its north and Buffalo Gap to its south selling alcohol, Abilene became known as "the city that was wet on both ends and dry in the middle." But these events marked only the beginning—Abilene's dry status, fictitious though it may have been, was on its last legs.

CIVIC IMPROVEMENTS

Although Abilenians disagreed, often vehemently, over alcohol sales, they found themselves more united on other issues. The city's dynamic growth during the 1950s created new needs that eventually had to be addressed. Census figures for 1960 indicated that Abilene's population had almost doubled during the previous decade, passing the 90,000 plateau. This reflected new arrivals lured by post-war economic expansion and Dyess Air Force Base, and, of course, the phenomenon known as the "Baby Boom." New housing, schools, stores, utilities, and social services would be required to support what had become a rather large town.

Above: Abilenians welcome the first B-1 bomber to arrive at Dyess Air Force Base in 1985. The rakish B-1 flew its first major combat missions in 1999.

COURTESY ABILENE REPORTER-NEWS.

Below: The workhorse C-130. Dyess-based C-130s yearly contribute to airlift operations worldwide. This retired plane is part of the outstanding exhibit at Dyess AFB's Linear Air Park.

COURTESY DAVID COFFEY.

The Taylor County Coliseum, now part of the expanded Expo Center, has hosted performers ranging from KISS to Lawrence Welk; Elvis Presley played Abilene in 1974. Most recently, the coliseum served as home ice for the short-lived Abilene Aviators hockey club.

COURTESY DAVID COFFEY.

Abilenians responded by not only addressing immediate concerns but also by showing considerable foresight. Cooper High School opened in the early 1960s, creating an instant cross-town rivalry with Abilene High. Other school systems such as the Wylie Independent School District would expand to address the population growth beyond Abilene's southern limits. The city's three universities also engaged in major building projects and campus improvements. New suburban shopping centers mirrored national trends. A series of major bond issues provided funding for a new courthouse, a new city hall, the Abilene Zoo, the downtown Civic Center, and the Taylor County Coliseum. The Coliseum, a major component of what would become the Expo Center of Taylor County, provided a venue for large concerts in the 1970s, including packed shows by performers as divergent as the Lawrence Welk Orchestra and the rock group KISS; in 1974 Elvis Presley played to a sold-out crowd. Abilene's enhanced infrastructure made it an attractive convention destination as well as a regional entertainment center that continues to draw huge crowds for the West Texas Fair and Rodeo, the Western Heritage Classic, and numerous equestrian events.

The railroad had made Abilene possible in the first place, and transportation continued to play a major role in the city's ability to grow and develop as a regional center. But with the advent of the Interstate highway system in the 1950s, and specifically the completion of Interstate 20, which linked Abilene to Fort Worth and Dallas by high-speed, multi-lane roadway, the complexion of transportation changed.

The T&P ended passenger rail service in the late 1960s, and by the mid-1970s the railroad that helped to create Abilene had been absorbed by the Missouri-Pacific (now the Union-Pacific). Air travel also changed the nature of Abilene's transportation services. Major upgrades at Abilene Regional Airport enabled the facility to attract jet passenger service during boom of the 1970s and 1980s. Jet service ended, and all but one major carrier ceased operations by the early 1990s, but, by the close of the decade, American Eagle added regional jet flights, with plans for expanded service, and other carriers prepared to enter the market.

Despite obvious development, Abilene rather languished in the '60s. A sluggish economy exacerbated by a decline in the oil business led to a slight decline in the city's population by the end of the decade. The malaise continued into the '70s, but Abilene found itself uniquely positioned to reap fabulous rewards when world events created a new oil boom.

THE OIL BOOM

For most of America, the 1970s became a bleak decade of double-digit inflation, high unemployment, and low production. Abilene was not immune to these economic ills, but events far away would lessen and in some cases erase their impact on the city—at least for a few good years. During the decline of the '60s, the major oil companies shut down their Abilene operations and prices for West Texas crude hovered around $3 a barrel. Government regulation and cheaper foreign oil prompted the majors to focus attention elsewhere—offshore, the Middle East, or Mexico for example. Only a few hearty independents remained. But the 1973 war in the Middle East resulted in an Arab oil embargo on nations that supported Israel in the conflict. This led to shortages, gas lines, rationing, and major price increases for domestic crude. It also brought the oil boom back to West Texas. When the crisis in Iran and Saudi production cutbacks sent prices toward the $40 a barrel level in 1979, Abilene boomed like never before.

Abilene became a center for the new boom. Stalwart independents were rewarded for their perseverance, and new companies flocked to the area. Exploration and production resumed at feverish levels, while oil field service operations hurried to keep pace. Would-be oil barons and laborers alike flocked to the area from around the

Nothing symbolized the Oil Boom better than the sprawling Fairway Oaks development on Abilene's south side, seen here in 1979.
COURTESY *ABILENE REPORTER-NEWS.*

country to cash in. In Abilene and statewide the oil boom ignited concurrent booms in banking, real estate, and construction. Locally, the effect proved dramatic, with long-lasting dividends.

Oil revenue spurred the development of the Fairway Oaks Golf and Racquet Club (and an associated residential addition) in south Abilene, which hosted the short-lived but lucrative LaJet Classic professional golf tournament, sponsored by one of Abilene's leading oil companies. The Petroleum Club had to expand to accommodate demand and still served packed houses daily. Southside growth and a vibrant economy led to the opening in 1979 of the Mall of Abilene, which brought five anchor retailers, restaurants, and a multi-screen movie theater. Local banks, real estate firms, and contractors expanded operations to previously unthinkable levels. The Texas oil business even provided source material for one of America's most popular television shows, *Dallas*. While most folks took exception to the outlandish characters on TV, some observers believed that the show hit home. In restaurants and clubs around Abilene, people met to make deals. They spent lavishly. Census figures for 1980 showed a population increase for Abilene of almost 10,000 people.

ABILENE GOES WET

The high-rolling times reinvigorated the wet/dry debate in Abilene. The city's few private clubs had all the business they could handle, and many new residents brought with them a desire for more available alcohol. Court decisions that allowed for wet precincts in otherwise dry counties had paved the way for places like Impact, but despite numerous attempts by pro-wet factions to bring a change, Abilene remained defiantly dry, holding to its traditional prohibition on the sale of alcoholic beverages—until 1978.

During the spring of 1978 pressure mounted as Abilenians on both sides of the issue marshaled support for a scheduled June 17 referendum. A group called Update '78 pressed for the legal sale, both on- and off-premises, of liquor, beer, and wine. Update '78 faced stiff competition from the Citizens for a Better Community (CBC), who carried the dry banner. A compromise group, the Citizens for Moderation, advanced the on-premise only option, or liquor-by-the-drink. Heated debate preceded the vote. In a true sign that times were changing, the *Abilene Reporter-News* endorsed the wet position. When the results came in the wets had carried the day by a margin of some 130 votes out of more than 23,000 cast. But the issue was not settled. The CBC challenged the results, which led to a divisive legal battle that threatened to tear the community apart. Finally, with church and university leaders calling for unity and understanding, the challenge was dropped. Beer trucks lined the highways into Abilene in anticipation. On September 20, beer went on sale at

business, the city celebrated the news that B-1B Lancers were coming to Dyess, which would keep the base off closure lists well into the future. An essentially stable population, solid retail and service industry sales, area universities and healthcare centers, and a burgeoning convention and tourism business helped ease the "hangover" from the oil boom. The city's population actually grew substantially during the '80s, passing the magical 100,000 mark. The 1990 census showed a population of more that 106,000. Indeed, Abilene emerged from the boom/bust cycle bigger and better than ever.

A massive revitalization of downtown, spurred by generous philanthropic efforts, began during the 1980s with the restoration of the classic 1930-vintage Paramount Theater. Development centered on North 1st and Cypress Streets, where the abandoned and decrepit Drake Hotel (originally the elegant Hotel Grace built in 1909) was transformed into the grand Grace Museum, which houses a variety of exhibits. Other renovations included the Cypress Building, and the old T&P warehouse and depot along North 1st Street. The abandoned Windsor Hotel, a former Hilton property, received a new life as a low-cost apartment building. Also slated for renovation was the Abilene Towers structure, once the majestic Wooten Hotel, and a host of other sites in and around downtown.

The Grace heads an impressive list of museums and cultural attractions that serve community

Above: A growing population and a booming economy encouraged the construction of the Mall of Abilene, seen here in an aerial shot prior to its opening in 1978. The regional attraction houses a variety of retail stores, restaurants, and entertainment establishments.

COURTESY ABILENE REPORTER-NEWS.

Right: The Paramount, restored to its 1930s Moorish splendor during the 1980s, draws large crowds to downtown for a variety of entertainment events, including weekend showings of classic movies.

COURTESY DAVID COFFEY.

local convenience stores. Liquor stores and new restaurants followed.

THE BUST THAT WASN'T

The boom and bust of the oil business struck with unmistakable vengeance in the 1980s. Deregulation had led to domestic overproduction at a time when the Organization of Petroleum Exporting Countries (OPEC) opted to drop its prices in response to global competition. The price of Texas crude began to tumble from the $40 a barrel plateau. Then, in the mid-1980s, OPEC dropped its production controls and flooded the world market, and the price for Texas oil plummeted to $10 a barrel. The boom was over.

Across the state, banks failed, real estate developments went uncompleted, companies folded in droves. Abilene felt the bust acutely, but had hedged against disaster.

Abilene found its salvation in its diversity. About the time the bottom fell out of the oil

and an increasing number of visitors. Downtown offers the Paramount Theater, the Center for Contemporary Arts, while the Abilene Zoo continues to add new animals and exhibits. Dyess AFB's Linear Air Park displays some thirty military aircraft from World War II to the present. Nearby attractions include Albany's Old Jail Art Center, Buffalo Gap Historic Village, and the Texas Forts Trail, headquartered in Abilene, which provides a link to the region's frontier past at sites such as Fort Phantom Hill, Fort Griffin, and Fort Chadbourne.

CONSOLIDATION

The 1990s became a time of consolidation for Abilene as the city continued to adjust to economic and social trends. Agriculture and oil continued to shape the city's identity and still contributed to the area's growing economy, but manufacturing, retail, and healthcare took larger shares than before. Dyess AFB remained an integral part of the picture. Abilene's four institutions of higher learning—Abilene Christian University, Hardin-Simmons University, McMurry University, and Cisco Junior College, which began classes in Abilene in the 1970s—boasted a combined enrollment of some 10,000 students in 1999.

The 1990s also witnessed a tremendous surge in sports and entertainment. The decade brought to town dozens of new restaurants, clubs, and recreational facilities, as well as a

state-of-the-art movie theater. But for a region steeped in football, the '90s held some surprising changes.

High school sports, especially football, have always been the main spectator attraction in West Texas and will likely remain so for decades to come. Abilene area teams routinely play to large crowds and with notable success. And Abilene's three universities continue to produce highly competitive teams and individual athletes. But during the 1990s two professional sports teams tested the waters—both failed, but for different reasons.

The Abilene Prairie Dogs, a minor league baseball franchise in the fledgling Texas-Louisiana League, at times fielded an attractive product at ACU's Crutcher Scott Field. But a lack

❖

Above: One enduring image of 1978's controversial wet/dry vote is the sight of beer trucks parked outside city limits as distributors awaited the go-ahead for beer sales at Abilene convenience stores.

COURTESY ABILENE REPORTER-NEWS.

Below: Abilenians flocked to local convenience stores in September 1978 to buy beer or simply to observe the spectacle. The novelty soon passed.

COURTESY ABILENE REPORTER-NEWS.

of fan support doomed the team in 1999. Poor fan support, though, could not be blamed for the failure of Abilene's other professional team.

However unlikely it might have seemed, ice hockey created huge excitement when it came to Abilene in 1998. The Abilene Aviators of the Western Professional Hockey League played to large, enthusiastic crowds at the Taylor County Coliseum, winning their division before losing in the playoffs. But ownership problems and fiscal mismanagement toppled the franchise during the 1999-2000 season.

While sports fans retain hope that professional hockey or baseball will return, some observers maintain that Abilene's approach to professional sports must change for that to happen. Again, alcohol is at the center of the debate. Beer sales were not allowed at either venue, which, critics charge, impacted fan turnout and denied owners a lucrative revenue stream. Yet another wet/dry conflict may confront Abilenians in the future.

From the beginning, having something to drink and enough of it, water for the most part, has been a driving concern for Abilenians. As the city enters the new millennium, that concern remains. A drought in the last years of the 1990s prompted water

rationing and left city leaders searching for ways to guarantee Abilene's water supply into the next century and beyond.

But droughts, like most aspects of life (including the oil business), are cyclical things—events to be endured and learned from. So as they have always done, Abilenians will adjust, learn, and act in order to keep the city alive and prosperous. The future has never looked brighter.

❖

A revitalized Downtown Abilene (top to bottom): the Grace Museum, the Paramount Theater, and the old T&P Depot, which now houses the Abilene Convention and Visitors Bureau and the Abilene Cultural Affairs Council.

TOP AND BOTTOM COURTESY DAVID COFFEY.
MIDDLE COURTESY *ABILENE REPORTER-NEWS*.

Cypress Street in the 1950s.

SHARING THE HERITAGE

historic profiles of

businesses and organizations

that have contributed to

the development and

economic base of Abilene

SPECIAL THANKS TO

CCC Supply

ELLIOTT-HAMIL FUNERAL HOMES

John A. (Pete) Elliott moved to Abilene in 1929, one year after graduating from the Dallas School of Embalming. He married the former Mittie Higginbotham in 1932. They opened Elliott's Funeral Home in 1933. This was considered a bold move by many in the Abilene community who were skeptical of the survival of new businesses during the era of the Great Depression. Times were not easy for the Elliotts. Two funeral cars, which they had ordered, sat on a railroad car for days because they did not have enough money to get them off. Thanks to the generosity of the J. M. Radfords, however, they were finally able to retrieve them for use.

In order to be available to the community at all times, Pete and Mittie chose to build their own home next door to the funeral home located at Orange and North 2nd Street. It was not unusual for people to knock on their door at all hours when assistance was needed. Not only did the Elliotts offer funeral service; they also provided ambulance service to the Abilene community.

When a death occurred, Pete and Mittie would prepare the body and then return the deceased to his home. Upon arrival home, friends and family members would gather to "sit up" with the body until the time of the service. Mittie would return later with fresh cake and coffee for the mourners. In those days, friends dug the graves and filled them following services.

At a time when few people were left unaffected by the ravages of the Depression, many people did not have the ability to pay a funeral director for his services. However, that did not prevent Pete and Mittie from providing funerals to them. Still, many families insisted on fulfilling their financial obligations to the Elliotts and did so in the form of goats, chickens, or pigs.

Mittie gave birth to a daughter, Jo Ann, shortly after she and Pete founded the funeral home. In 1939, Mittie received her funeral directors license. During World War II, Jo Ann

Top: John A. (Pete) Elliott.

Right: Elliott's Funeral Home at North 2nd and Orange, circa 1935.

After working as an ambulance carrier for many years, Pete helped to bring air ambulance service to the Abilene area. He even obtained his own commercial pilot's license. He loved to fly and fostered the same spirit in his daughter who learned to fly as well.

In 1947, Elliott's Funeral Home moved to its present location at 542 Hickory Street. It had been the Batjer family home. The Elliotts added a chapel to the original structure and made other modifications, as they were financially able to do so.

In 1950, the family moved to a home on the outskirts of Abilene. Pete loved nature and working with his hands. Here, Pete was able to keep goats, chickens, and other livestock including an old mule. After working at the funeral home all day, Pete spent hours tirelessly plowing his fields with his mule, Jethro, and grinding corn at his grist mill. His cornmeal was known area-wide.

After Jo Ann graduated from Abilene High School in 1953, she decided to follow in her parents' professional footsteps. She attended the Dallas Institute of Mortuary Science, where she was only one of two women in her class. In 1958, Jo Ann married John Hamil, who was also a funeral director. Together, the Elliotts and the young Hamils worked to uphold the standards of excellence first established by Pete and Mittie.

In spite of a somewhat demanding schedule at the funeral home, the young Hamils decided

remembered her father waiting at the depot to meet the escorts and receive the caskets of Abilene men—many who were just boys—who had gone off to fight. In particular, she recalled the crash of a plane in which twenty-six people were killed. The Elliotts opened their home to the Air Force and the families as identification of the dead went on for days. When a ship carrying ammonium nitrate burst into flames in the port of Texas City, Pete gathered his gear and responded to the call for help. More than 500 people were killed in the fiery disaster.

Top: Mittie Elliott.

Left: Elliott's Funeral Home at 542 Hickory Street in the early 1950s.

Above: John and Jo Ann Hamil.

Top, right: Robert E. Hamil.

to begin a family of their own. In 1963, their first child, a daughter, Cynthia, was born. Then another daughter, Angela, was born in 1964. And, finally, they welcomed a son, Robert, in 1965. Pete was a proud grandfather, who often scooped up all three small grandchildren for daily outings in his old pickup.

Pete, a past president of the Texas Funeral Directors Association (TFDA), visited every funeral home in the state. On his journeys he collected photos and other memorabilia. His wish was to erect a building in Austin, which would house the offices of the Texas Funeral Directors Association and the State Board of Morticians as well as a funeral service museum.

When Pete died prematurely at the age of sixty-three, John continued working to fulfill Pete's dream. After his death, Mittie, John, and Jo Ann carried on the tradition of dedicated service at the funeral home that the Elliotts had established so many years before. Remaining true to that tradition, Mittie proudly continued working at the funeral home until the time of her death at the age of eighty-nine in 1994.

In an effort to handle the increasing needs of a growing city, the family built another funeral home on Highway 277 in 1974. At that time, the name was changed to Elliott-Hamil Funeral Homes. The decade of the 1970s brought with it much change—not only for the city of Abilene but for the funeral business as well. Families were scattered across the country and, in some cases, around the world. This complicated funeral arrangements. State legislation increased paperwork for funeral homes. However, this did not deter the Elliott-Hamil family. As they successfully adapted to the ever-changing business world, they were mindful of the spirit on which Elliott-Hamil was originally built. They remembered to do business with compassion, kindness, and grace.

In the early '80s, John Hamil's health began to fail. Beset with renal failure and frustrated with pain, John was still determined to serve the

needs of his community. John scheduled his dialysis treatments to accommodate his responsibilities at the funeral home. In spite of his illness, he and Jo Ann continued to work side-by-side just as the Elliotts had before them.

John once had a dream of seeing a cemetery established on acreage surrounding the funeral home on Highway 277. He worked diligently to make that happen. His dream became a reality when he opened the Elliott-Hamil Garden of Memories there in 1996. When he died in 1998, a standing-room-only crowd turned out to honor his memory.

Today, Jo Ann Elliott-Hamil and her son, Robert, manage all funeral home and cemetery operations together with assistance from her daughter, Angela, each carrying on the family tradition.

Above: The Elliott-Hamil Funeral Home location at 542 Hickory.

Below: Elliott-Hamil Funeral Home and Garden of Memories Cemetery at 5701 U.S. Highway 277 South.

HENDRICK HEALTH SYSTEM

❖

Right: Over the last seventy-five years, Hendrick Health System has grown to meet the healthcare needs of the Texas Midwest. This picture was taken in 1943 shortly after a new wing had been added.

Below: Technological advancements in medical equipment have been ever changing since Hendrick opened its doors in 1924 as the West Texas Baptist Sanitarium. Depicted here is an early operating room used at the hospital.

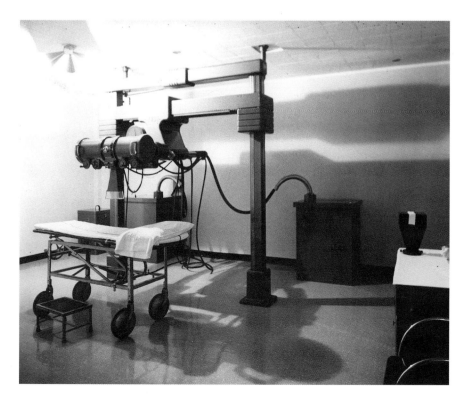

West Texas Baptist Sanitarium began as a dream in the hearts and minds of a group of committed Christians. Seeing the physical and emotional illnesses around them, they took seriously Christ's charge to "Preach the Kingdom of God and to heal the sick." (Luke 9:2) They realized that Christian compassion and medical science could work together in helping sick and hurting people, and they struggled to bring a hospital to the Texas Midwest.

Hendrick Health System opened September 15, 1924 as West Texas Baptist Sanitarium with seventy-five beds, five stories, hot and cold running water in each room, three modern elevators, an excellent nursing service, efficient laboratory services, a well-equipped obstetrical department, and a staff of capable surgeons and physicians.

During the Great Depression, the debt-ridden hospital had a difficult struggle to keep its doors open. In 1936, Mr. and Mrs. T. G. Hendrick paid off the hospital's debts and added fifty beds. In gratitude, the hospital was named Hendrick Memorial Hospital.

Through the 1940s and '50s, wings and floors were added to the central core. In 1963, the Minnie L. Anderson Building was constructed and in 1966, the Malcolm and Mary Meek Building. The Collier Wing was completed in 1971, housing surgery, intensive and coronary care units, and medical/surgical units.

In 1974, Hendrick Health System Foundation's Campaign '80 raised $4 million for continued Hendrick growth. In 1977, the hospital was renamed Hendrick Health System and the Professional Center and Residential Retirement Center opened. In the 1980s, doors opened for two projects, the Mabee Building, housing a new Emergency Department and admission area; and the Southeast Wing, housing administration, laboratory, and physical therapy.

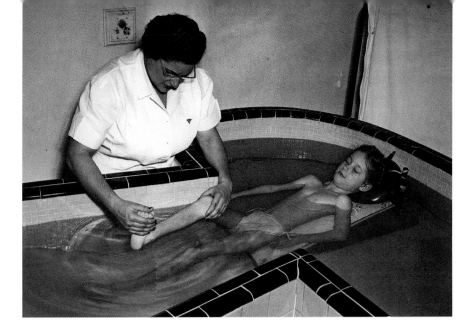

The 1980s were a time of tremendous growth, including a new mothercare and labor/delivery unit, an inpatient cancer treatment center, new critical care unit, the Hendrick League House and Mesa Springs Retirement Village and Nursing Home. The momentum continued into the '90s with the Meadows Conference Center for the Abilene Intercollegiate School of Nursing; a fixed site for magnetic resonance imaging and a new facility for the Meek Community Blood Bank and Pathology Consultants, and, thanks to the support of the Children's Miracle Network Telethon, a pediatric intermediate care unit.

In the 1990s, Hendrick Health System continued to expand services in all aspects of the healthcare field. In 1993, Hendrick Heartsaver Network was completed with the addition of open-heart surgery. Hendrick Center for Rehabilitation opened in August 1993, providing inpatient rehabilitation medicine for Abilene and surrounding counties. Hendrick also completed its spectrum of retirement living services in 1993 when it acquired Hendrick Wisteria Place, an assisted living facility. In 1994, Hendrick added new dimensions to its emergency services: First Flight, an air ambulance service, and a Chest Pain Emergency Department.

In 1995, new additions to Hendrick services included a Pediatric Intensive Care Unit, sub-acute rehabilitation program and the electro-physiology procedure—a procedure where defective heart muscle is actually burned and destroyed to eliminate heartbeat irregularities.

Hendrick Health Place, an educational center located in the Mall of Abilene was opened to the public in 1997. Free learning seminars, health screenings and events are just some of the services the public can receive at Hendrick Health Place.

The Vera West Women's Center, opened in 1998, which brought a new freestanding women's center named for long-time community member Vera West. This facility houses physicians affiliated with Hendrick Women's Network, a radiology department and a resource center. The services available at the center help women at every stage of life from new moms to women concerned about osteoporosis or menopause.

In 1999, the Shelton Building named after Stormy Shelton was dedicated. The Shelton Building houses Hendrick Cancer Center, the Auxiliary Conference Center and the Farrington Room dedicated to the use of telemedicine technology. The Shelton Building is available to the community for events or educational opportunities. Additions to the Cath Lab and a new Cardiovascular Operating Room were also dedicated during 1999.

Hendrick Health System is proud to offer the best available services and technology to the community members of the Texas Midwest. As we continue to grow and expand services, so does our commitment to patient care and community education, making Hendrick the first name in healthcare.

Above: In the 1950s the medical staff at Hendrick saw many post polio patients. This young patient is receiving a whirlpool treatment by a physical therapist. Although the whirlpool is still used in treatment, the general use is now for wound care and burn patients. PHOTO COURTESY OF THURMAN'S STUDIO.

Below: The first Iron Lung was developed in 1929. It gained wide usage during the polio epidemic, however, some patients still use Iron Lungs in their homes today. Most patients, however, use various ventilators to help with their respiratory needs.

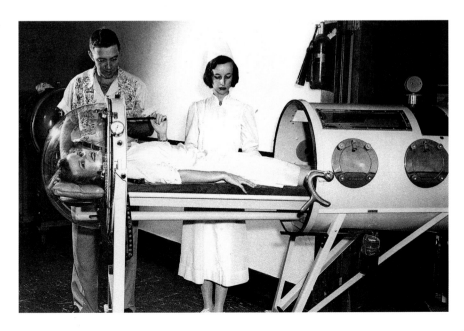

THE LEGEND OF THE BLACK-EYED PEA

In Abilene, the summer of 1935 was more than hot and dry. It was devastating.

The Great Depression and the worst drought the area had ever seen combined to cripple the entire region. Farmers, ranchers and merchants were all without money. Everything was cheap, but it didn't really matter. No one had any money to purchase anything anyway.

Hendrick, at that time named West Texas Baptist Sanitarium, was one of the institutions suffering the most. The depression had increased the need for charity work, and, at the same time, rendered the churches too feeble to support the hospital.

There was no money to pay the electric bill or to purchase food for patients and employees. The dire circumstances made it almost certain the hospital would close its doors. E. M. Collier, the young and aggressive administrator of the fledgling ten-year-old hospital, sent out a cry of desperation to West Texans for any help they might be able to muster.

Hospital employees were the first to respond. Many took only enough money out of their paychecks to pay for their families' essentials. Others turned their entire paychecks back to the hospital to help in keeping the doors open.

In the dry June of 1935, only one crop appeared to thrive—black-eyed peas. Employees began bringing bushels of peas to the hospital, and, before long, farmers from Lueders, Avoca, Potosi, Buffalo Gap, Merkel, Clyde, and other surrounding towns began to arrive with pick-ups filled with bushels of peas.

Collier perched himself at the entrance of the hospital greeting patients and shelling peas. Nurses shelled peas at nursing stations throughout the hospital. Orderlies and housekeepers finished their duties early and spent their remaining hours shelling peas.

Big vats of peas were cooked in the hospital kitchen, and black-eyed peas, served with cornbread and mush, became the dietary staple for patients, employees, and physicians.

Collier, who served West Texas Baptist Sanitarium and Hendrick for more than forty years, saw the hospital through this most difficult time. However, he never forgot the "Black-eyed Pea Summer of 1935."

"That summer taught us to never underestimate the value of even the smallest thing," Mr. Collier said years later. "I don't think we would have survived without someone thinking to give us that first bushel of peas…and then the bushels just kept coming. It was a wonderful time for the hospital."

In the early 1970s, historic preservation was almost unknown in West Texas because people did not think anything was old enough to be considered historic. By 1975, however, a small, dedicated group of volunteers recognized that much of Abilene's heritage was in danger of being lost. From this concern, the Abilene Preservation League was formed.

The APL is committed to preserving properties deemed architecturally and historically significant. Its purpose is to educate and obtain community support to benefit historic preservation. Early in its history, APL focused on educating the public about the need for and the economic benefits of historic preservation. Later efforts centered on implementing its goals such as helping the city adopt the ordinance that created the Landmarks Commission and historic overlay zoning.

In that time, such significant structures as Paramount Theater, the Grace Cultural Center and the Compton Building have been saved and restored, creating a dynamic, economically viable downtown with the T&P Historic District as its focal point. Residential areas such as Sayles Boulevard and the Parramore Historic District have undergone revitalization and were placed on the National Register of Historic Places. One of the last great mansions, the Swenson House, has been saved and maintained as a community resource. Other APL projects include efforts to protect, restore, and reuse the Elks Lodge building and Abilene's oldest church, St. Francis Catholic Church.

Throughout its history, APL has been recognized for its efforts and has received the Texas Historical Commission's Texas Award for its Historic Landmark Survey; Texas Society of Architects Citation of Honor; American Planning Association's Urban Design Award for the Grace Cultural Center; Texas Historical Foundation's Citation of Merit; and the Texas Historical Commission's Award of Excellence.

The Abilene Preservation League relies on the community in its efforts to make Abilene a significant West Texas city. Through membership in the organization and support of its fundraisers such as Celebrate Abilene! and the annual tour of historic homes, Abilenians help ensure the continuity of our historic resources for future generations.

ABILENE PRESERVATION LEAGUE

Top: Colonel Clabe Merchant's home was built in 1881 shortly after Abilene's town lot sale. The home was located on the site of Merchant Park Shopping Center. It was razed in 1956. It's image serves as the Abilene Preservation League's logo.

Right: The 1913 Elks Lodge Building will serve as an art center and the home of the Abilene Preservation League.

WEST TEXAS UTILITIES COMPANY

West Texas Utilities Company is truly a pioneer business firm. The founding of the company can be traced back to about 1891; the first year there were electric lights in Abilene.

Seven years after Thomas Edison built his famous Pearl Street Station, J. G. Lowden and Otto Steffens built a small generating plant in Abilene to furnish electricity to a few customers. These customers were served mainly in the after-noons and evenings, providing lights for stores and modern conveniences for the housewife. Also, every drugstore had to have a "new fangled" electric cigar lighter. Customers were charged according to the number of light bulbs and appliances they had rather than being metered.

Lowden and Steffens sold the company to a group of Abilene businessmen who expanded the business to include a power and ice plant and a water company along with the electric distribution system. Two companies were formed, one to supply electricity and water and the other to furnish ice.

These businesses soon attracted the attention of an eastern business giant, the American Public Service Company. In December of 1912, the American Public Service Company bought all the utility firms in Abilene including the streetcar company.

The company took the name of Abilene Gas and Electric Company and provided service in Abilene and Merkel. Between 1912 and 1922, many small isolated utilities over West Texas were added to the system.

In 1923, the company began electric operations under the name of West Texas Utilities Company and acquired several other existing facilities, including the company owned Roby and Northern Railroad. The railroad was a 4½-

mile-line running from Roby to the Katy Railroad Junction at North Roby.

WTU acquired the San Angelo properties in 1924, including Miles, Rowena, Ballinger, Winters, and Hatchell. Central and South West Utilities Company was founded in 1925 to manage the extensive properties that would eventually become the Central and South West System (CSW), including WTU. In 1926, twenty-four towns were added to the list of towns being served by West Texas Utilities Company. WTU established a record growth in 1927, by adding thirty-six towns and almost 1,000 miles of transmission lines.

WTU acquired the Dalhart Public Service Company in 1931 and the Big Bend District in 1945, however government regulations later required the sale of the Dalhart District.

Today, WTU is a Central and South West Company and serves 170 towns and communities in fifty-two counties, extending from the Red River to the Rio Grande, an area of 53,000 square miles.

In addition to West Texas Utilities Company, CSW now has domestic and international holdings that include Central Power and Light Company in Corpus Christi, Public Service Company of Oklahoma in Tulsa, Southwestern Electric Power Company in Shreveport, and Seeboard in the United Kingdom. Other subsidiaries include CSW Energy, Inc., CSW International, Inc., CSW Communications, Inc., CSW Credit, Inc., Enershop Inc. and Central and South West Services, Inc.

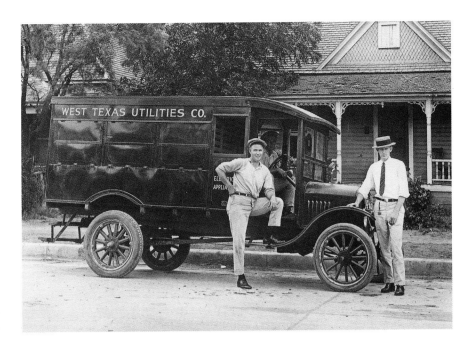

❖

Top: Electric appliance delivery truck, 1922-1923.

Above: Roby & Northern Railway at Roby, Texas, 1925.

Left: Reddy Kilowatt was on the job promoting safety as early as the 1940s or 1950s.

ABILENE REGIONAL MEDICAL CENTER

West Texas Medical Center, the predecessor institution for Abilene Regional Medical Center, was originally built in 1968 by a group of Abilene physicians and investors on East Highway 80. It soon became known for its innovative cardiovascular services. The hospital's Heart Team performed Texas Midwest's first heart catheterization in 1970, followed by the area's first open-heart surgery.

In 1984, David Collins, chief executive officer from 1969-1994, and his team moved the hospital to its replacement facility and new home on a thirty-three-acre campus in South Abilene, now the city's high growth area. The original WTMC facility was donated to the City of Abilene.

In 1992, the two-story, 30,000-square-foot Abilene Heart & Vascular Institute opened, reaching out to the public with education, and screening and assessment tools to help them reduce risk factors for cardiovascular disease. The Institute's Center for Referral Services added a pediatric cardiology clinic in 1996, and real-time review of diagnostic imaging via its new telemedicine capability in 1999.

Now, thirty years later, ARMC's success rate for open-heart surgery is 99.2 percent, better than area, state, and national averages. Cardiovascular procedures represent more than forty percent of ARMC's patient care. Domination of the area's cardiovascular market resulted from the skill of our experienced, dedicated Heart Team of cardiovascular and thoracic surgeons, cardiologists, nurses, and technicians.

"Cardiovascular services are our strong suit," said Woody F. Gilliland, chief executive officer from 1994-2000. "But in today's healthcare environment, we are looked to as a provider of a variety of services, especially for women's health, and we are constantly growing to meet patient demands."

Abilene Regional Medical Center has grown to be a comprehensive healthcare system anchored by its 187-bed hospital. It serves a seventeen-county service area population of 325,000, offering patients a full continuum of acute care in inpatient and outpatient services, provided by more than 250 staff physicians, representing forty-four areas of medical specialization, and 850 employees. Recently added hospital-based services include complete oncology care through our collaboration with Texas Cancer Center, rehabilitation services through our partnership with West Texas Rehabilitation Center, a dedicated Pediatrics Unit, Wound Care Center, and designation of our Emergency Department as a certified Trauma Center by the Texas Department of Health.

Your Women's Center, a $15.6 million expansion project, opened in the summer of 1999. Your Women's Center provides more private rooms for patients, expanded and renovated Intensive Care Units, a Neonatal Special Care Unit expanded to twelve isolettes, a new sixteen-bed Well-Baby Nursery, and sixteen All-In-One-Room Birthing Suites, where as many as 150 infants are born every month.

"ARMC's employees and physicians have worked very hard over the years to develop our reputation as a healthcare leader," Gilliland said. "We're working just as hard now to continue providing patient-centered healthcare that exceeds the expectations of those we serve, well into the twenty-first century."

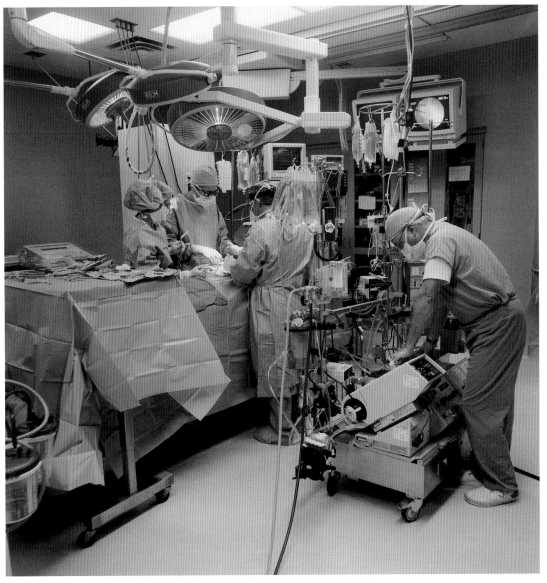

DODGE JONES FOUNDATION

At 10:00 a.m. on Christmas Day, 1954, the first meeting of the board of directors of the Dodge Jones Foundation was convened at the Fort Worth Club. Present were Ruth Legett Jones and her daughters, Julia (Judy) Jones Matthews and Edith Jones O'Donnell. Envisioning a charitable foundation named for the only male Jones sibling, Dodge, who died as a young man in the 1940s, these women, the widow and daughters of Percy Jones began a philanthropy that in so many ways reflects the personalities of both families' ancestry, as well as their own strong beliefs.

The Texas connection for the Jones families dates back to May 15, 1866 when Colonel Morgan Jones, a Welshman, arrived in New York City from Liverpool and began working on the rapidly expanding railroad system of the western United States. He developed what was to be a lifelong friendship with General Grenville Dodge, the officer to whom President Lincoln gave the responsibility of keeping the railroads running during the Civil War. Colonel Jones never married and, over a period of time, brought his three nephews to the U.S. to help him operate his railroad construction business, which had moved beyond Texas into Kansas and Colorado. Percy, the second to arrive, while never having known Dodge, eventually named his only son after the general when requested to do so by his uncle, affectionately known as the "Old Mahn."

Ruth Legett Jones' Texas legacy is equally as strong. Her father, Judge K. K. Legett of Abilene, helped establish Simmons College (now Hardin-Simmons University), writing its by-laws and serving on the founding board. He also served eight years on the board of Texas A&M, four of those as President. Vernon Gladden Spence, a historian who met Mrs. Jones while writing his biography of Colonel Jones, was so intrigued with her and the stories of her mother and maternal grandmother that he wrote a second volume, *Pioneer Women of Abilene: A Trilogy*. In the foreword to that book, Katharyn Duff chose such terms as extraordinary, discerning, compassionate, intelligent, and sensitive to describe this very "private gentlewoman."

Top: The Jones Family, 1936. Clockwise from left: Julia (Judy), Percy, Ruth, Dodge, and Edith.

Below: A new locomotive for the Abilene and Southern Railroad, September 1926.

Members of both sides of this remarkable family, including the Colonel, sought no attention for their activities. Indeed, Mrs. Jones viewed the Foundation as a means of allowing her to perform charitable work in a quiet manner. She held deep concerns for the black population in her city; building a neighborhood pool, beginning a day nursery, and helping a number of black children go to college.

As its philanthropic scope has expanded during recent years under the leadership and guidance of President Julia Jones Matthews, the Foundation has also extended its giving to a wider range of West Texas from which much of its oil-based resources are derived, and beyond.

Areas of interest include the development of medical programs and the preservation of significant historical sites. The restoration of the old Grace Hotel was especially meaningful since Colonel Jones often made it his residence when in Abilene. Education has also been a primary focus with projects running the gamut from early childhood development and latchkey children programs to the development of a nursing school consortium among three local universities, as well as a citywide library consortium.

Through all the effort, the quiet style of philanthropy has remained constant. Gifts are generally made anonymously. The board feels that it is those whose good work is being rewarded who should be recognized, not the donor. One of the principal prototypes of the Foundation's commitment to the empowerment of others was the seminal grant for the Community Foundation of Abilene in 1985; a gift made with the hope of influencing others to invest in giving.

The specific reason for the first meeting of the Dodge Jones Foundation Board of Directors being held on Christmas morning in a private club in downtown Fort Worth has long since been forgotten. But it was a Christmas the Jones family spent with their thoughts of Percy and Dodge; it was the gathering of three women who had lost a husband and father, a son, and a brother. The creation of the Dodge Jones Foundation that winter morning, whether arising from a sense of mourning or celebration, has certainly been a blessing to the people of Texas for the past four and a half decades.

❖

Left: Percy Jones, age sixty-five, 1950.

Right: Ruth Jones, age eighty-five, 1978.

ABILENE DIAGNOSTIC CLINIC

Dr. Zane Travis is one of the eight physicians who founded Abilene Diagnostics, which is the predecessor of Abilene Diagnostic Clinic. Dr. Travis said he had come through Abilene on his way home to Houston for a visit while he was in service on a New Mexico Indian reservation.

"My wife and I liked the people," he said, "and we had stopped for coffee in a drug store, and Dr. Turnbull was there. I asked him if Abilene could use an internist. He said yes, they could use about ten. That reinforced our desire to live here."

Abilene Diagnostic Clinic originally began in the late 1960s as an outgrowth of a partnership between Dr. Travis and Dr. Edward Martin. They soon added two cardiologists and formed a cardiology clinic, which later brought in more physicians and eventually they built a clinic that was named Abilene Diagnostics.

Abilene Diagnostics opened its first clinic on East Highway 80 in a plant that the old West Texas Medical Center had constructed for extended care. About fifteen years later, they opened another building adjacent to Abilene Regional Medical Center (called Humana at the time). Abilene Diagnostic Clinic then migrated across the highway to a newly built facility known as the Medical Mall of Abilene.

In 1995, Abilene Diagnostic Clinic was formed as a new entity uniting fourteen former solo practitioners who were looking for a way to maintain their patient-centered practices with emphasis on the individuals, while dealing with the new politics of corporate medicine. By forming an

Top: Dr. Ed Martin was co-founder with Dr. Zane Travis of the first Abilene Diagnostic Clinic.

Right: Space-age technology is among Abilene Diagnostic Clinic's arsenal of diagnostic tools.

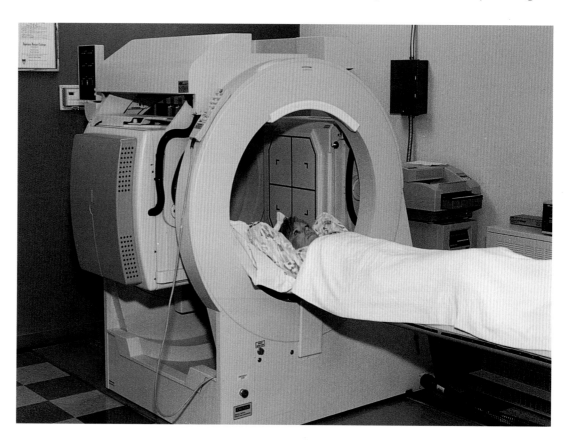

alliance, they could share resources and information systems enabling them to provide better healthcare for the people of Abilene, thus allowing the group the ability to negotiate with managed care and insurance companies. The new consortium quickly drew in other local physicians and within a few short months had grown to a total of forty-three doctors, focusing on family care, but also taking in such practices as pediatrics, obstetrics/gynecology, neurology, urology, surgery, anesthesia, and pain management.

Patients of Abilene Diagnostic Clinic physicians enjoy not only the advantage of the highest quality care at fair costs, but the benefits of timely information gathered through space-age diagnostic tools that are available onsite at the clinic. Abilene Diagnostic Clinic offers complete Medicare-approved lab facilities, stress tests, X-ray, and nuclear medicine—all services under one roof. A patient experiencing problems can go to an Abilene Diagnostic Clinic physician, then have all tests and lab work done without leaving the clinic, and in most cases, learn the results of the tests the same day.

"We're able to get more done for our patients with much less of a hassle," said Dr. David Bailey. "If a patient comes in with chest pains, I can send them down for a stress test, lab work or X-ray and have it back immediately. In the old days, it would be two or three days before I had the results. Being a full service facility allows us to streamline our patients' healthcare."

Abilene Diagnostic Clinic is able to meet the patients' needs immediately. According to the physicians of Abilene Diagnostic Clinic, the alliance has met or surpassed their expectations.

Today, with facilities on both the north and south side of town, Abilene Diagnostic Clinic encompasses almost everything that primary care covers, and maintains a close referral relationship with physicians in other specialties. With twenty-six primary care physicians in the group, Abilene Diagnostic Clinic is also accessible to new patients looking for the best care possible—with doctors who will listen and care for them as individuals, and yet be able to offer the best and most advanced medical techniques available.

❖

Abilene Diagnostic Clinic provides complete diagnostic services under one roof.

OSI
SECURITY, INC.

OSI Security, which serves Abilene with armored car and guard and patrol service, began in 1978 when Jerry and Sandra Cannon quit their jobs, cashed in their retirement and savings and moved to Abilene to start an oilfield theft deterrent business.

As a Brownwood police officer, Jerry had learned a lot from interviews with both thieves and their victims. Sandra had been an office manager for a large mechanical contractor. She would be able to handle the business details and paperwork.

Although they were successful in getting oilfield theft investigations, they needed more work than they had. Plaintiff attorneys were doing a booming business, and soon they were knocking on the Cannon's door seeking Jerry's services. He applied for and received his private investigator's license because of his police background, and Sandra received her license on the strength of her prior experience in corrections at the State School. The money was good, but the Cannons decided they'd rather work on the other side of the fence. They began doing workmen compensation and insurance fraud investigations. Once Jerry paid a woman $20 to "rent" her bathroom for about five minutes while he photographed a plaintiff with a "back injury" as he carried shingles to

the top of the house next door, and replaced the roof. The man had gone to court in a wheelchair, but after seeing the Cannon photos, his attorney dropped the suit.

Another time, a plaintiff they were investigating who claimed he had sustained an accident that had left him in a wheelchair, took a cab to a local bar. Sandra took a barstool beside him, and when he asked her to dance, Jerry produced an 8-mm camera and recorded his miraculous recovery.

Meanwhile, they continued to do their oil field theft deterrent and investigative work. Jerry had learned from the contractors and oil operators he called on that even though stolen equipment could be traced, there was no way of proving ownership, since serial numbers could be easily filed off.

Jerry developed a two-phase system of identification, first stamping unique numbers onto the steel equipment and welding a protective ridge around them, then photographing and keeping files of each customer's equipment.

Then one day Jerry called on the comptroller of Pool Well Services. Although the comptroller wasn't interested in the system from a theft deterrent aspect, he had something else in mind. He offered to buy Jerry's method and then hire the Cannons to train a cadre of Pool

people to implement the identification process on every piece of equipment on Pool's 2,000 rigs. The Cannons, who had begun by traveling the oil field backroads in their 1979 Ford pickup with welding machine, camera, and portable typewriter, now trained others to do the work.

They got out of the oilfield theft deterrent business just ahead of a severe oil bust. They branched into patrol services, with Sandra making sales calls and doing office work during the day, and Jerry calling on customers and doing patrol work evenings. They bought two patrol cars, and hired people to patrol and to handle dispatch services. With the growth of the patrol service, the addition of burglar alarms was a natural next step. Jerry had a background in electronics, and did the alarm installations. OSI became certified, as Abilene's only Underwriters Laboratory-listed central station, which brought jewelry stores and banks in as customers. OSI offered its customers complete protection—installing alarms, monitoring them, and sending patrols around to check on them. But the paperwork was overwhelming.

"Everything back then was cards and papers," he remembers. "We had between 250 and 300 customers, and every time they turned the alarm on, it would send a signal, and every time they turned it off, it would send another signal. And each time, we had to fill out a time card and initial it. The answer to the problem lay in computerization. In 1983, OSI installed two TRS-80 Radio Shack computers with twenty megabyte hard drives and backups utilizing VHS tapes! As the only company in town with such a monitoring system and UL certification as well, OSI was soon serving competitors as well as its own customers.

In the latter part of 1982, with ATMs about to burst on the scene, and with the offer of a contract from Abilene National Bank, the Cannons placed an order with a company in Tennessee for two armored cars. However, on the day they were to sign the contract with Abilene National Bank, it announced that it had been bought out by BankOne and OSI's armored car service contract was off. Jerry Cannon put on his hat and drove downtown to First State Bank, which was also installing ATMs. There was one other

armored car service in town, but First State agreed to use OSI's service. Then the Cannons, having lost one contract and gained another in a week's time, went to work calling on other businesses, and soon had all the work they could do.

In 1986, they sold the alarm company, and about two months later, the other armored car service, citing lack of profitability, announced that it was pulling out of Abilene. Today, OSI is the only armored car service in town.

This means the Cannons are constantly improving their service, keeping on the cutting edge of safety and protection for their customers. "We're extremely happy to be a part of the Abilene business community, and we do our utmost to maintain their trust," says Jerry.

The Cannons have four children—all grown, with children of their own. One son lives in Abilene, another lives in Topeka, Kansas; another commutes between Abilene and Comanche, and a daughter lives in Lubbock.

OSI Security founders Jerry and Sandra Cannon.

BEN RICHEY BOYS RANCH

Ben Richey Boys Ranch, nearing the end of its fifty-second year, stands as a model for the troubled boy to learn values by observing Christians in action.

A private, nonprofit basic childcare facility, the Ranch is funded by the Abilene United Way, by periodic fundraisers, and other donations. It receives no federal funding. The Ranch provides the environment and opportunity for boys to grow, to become well educated, and to gain the confidence to function as good citizens who can make the right decisions. The story of the ranch shows how a community works together to make the right decisions in times of crisis.

The Ranch was begun by Ben Richey, a good, unassuming man who had left a lucrative traveling sales job and settled in Abilene in 1939 to spend more time with his family. Richey became a Scoutmaster, and began working with an Abilene youth boxing program. He was troubled to see many boys without Christian role models, repeated troublemakers who couldn't break the cycle of bad attitudes and bad actions that ended too often inside prison walls.

He appealed to the Abilene City Council with an idea for a boys' ranch similar to Father Flanagan's Boys Town, or Cal Farley's Boys Ranch near Amarillo.

In 1945, the Council dedicated 300 acres of city land adjacent to Lake Kirby for the development of a facility at an unspecified future date.

In 1946, Optimists International wanting his help to start a chapter in Abilene approached

Richey. He agreed, and proposed the boys ranch as their first project.

Richey and the newly organized Abilene Optimists obtained a charter for the Abilene Boys Ranch, then borrowed $2,400 to convert a Camp Barkeley barracks building to house eight boys and a Christian couple to act as houseparents. But after two sets of houseparents left within five months, Richey responded once again to the boys' needs by offering himself.

Mrs. Richey, who had to care for her blind mother, was unable to leave with her husband,

so Ben and his wife's brother, Edwin Yeager, packed up their clothes and moved to the Ranch to look after the boys until Mrs. Richey could come. It turned out to be a lifetime commitment for all three of them.

They could hardly have chosen a more difficult calling. In addition to the boys' ingrained attitude problems, there were always financial difficulties.

The Abilene Optimists withdrew their sponsorship in 1949. In 1950, the Richeys' and the younger boys' cottage burned. In 1952, the Abilene Jaycees, who had agreed to support the Ranch after the withdrawal of the Optimists, also withdrew. The Richeys sold their house and four acres of land in Abilene to pay Ranch debts of about $10,000.

Finances gradually got better, however, aided in large part by the Abilene Boys Ranch Board of Directors, hand-picked by Richey and named in 1954 for their generosity as well as their fundraising talents.

By the time Ben Richey died in 1973, the Ranch had grown a reputation for its quality of management as well as its success in turning around the lives of the boys who lived there.

After he died the Ranch declined, and community support diminished. For several years it floundered, but by 1984, the Ranch had begun to take on new vitality and new direction.

Strong accountability measures were taken to ensure proper management of the Ranch, while fundraisers canvassed the Big Country area to reintroduce the Ranch to the community and regain financial support. Soon, the Ranch was back on track, with remodeled and new facilities and equipment, and a staff energized and totally dedicated to the precepts Richey had espoused all his life. In 1987, the Board honored him posthumously by renaming the Ranch, Ben Richey Boys Ranch.

This profile was made possible by an anonymous Ranch friend.

Top: Celebrating Christmas at Ben Richey Boys Ranch.

Bottom: The Ranch provides the environment and opportunity for boys to grow, to become well educated, and to gain the confidence to function as good citizens who can make the right decisions.

First Baptist Church of Abilene

Abilene's First Baptist Church was organized December 17, 1881, under the aegis of Dr. Owen C. Pope, corresponding secretary and superintendent of the State Baptist Convention, and with the help of the Reverend T. R. Leggett, pastor of Buffalo Gap Baptist Church. There were seventeen members.

In February 1882, a building committee began to look for a site for a church house. The church bought a lot on the corner of North 4th and Cedar Streets for $50. In 1910, First Baptist built a larger church house at the corner of North 2nd and Hickory with a dining room and kitchen in the basement. It was four more years, however, before the street itself was paved. The north educational building was erected in 1929. The present sanctuary, which became the center around which other structures were added or bought to accommodate the church's growing membership, was built in 1954. Upon the sanctuary's completion, the church celebrated for an entire week around the theme, "The Church that Christ Built."

The south education building, constructed on the site of the former sanctuary, was dedicated in 1963. It included a new kitchen, dining room, and chapel. In 1979, First Baptist purchased the C&T building on North 2nd Street to house the

Ministry of Counseling and Enrichment and young adult Sunday School classes. The Family Life Center was built in 1981, and the church acquired University Place, at the corner of North 3rd and Hickory Streets, in 1982 for the use of the university ministry.

As a part of its most recent building campaign, beginning in 1994, the church built a new counseling center on North 1st, a new full-block parking lot between North 1st and North 2nd, paid off the church debt, and renovated much of the educational facilities.

Top: A sketch of the original First Baptist Church house built in 1883.

Right: The First Baptist Church at North Second and Hickory was built in 1910.

PHOTO COURTESY OF BOB JONES.

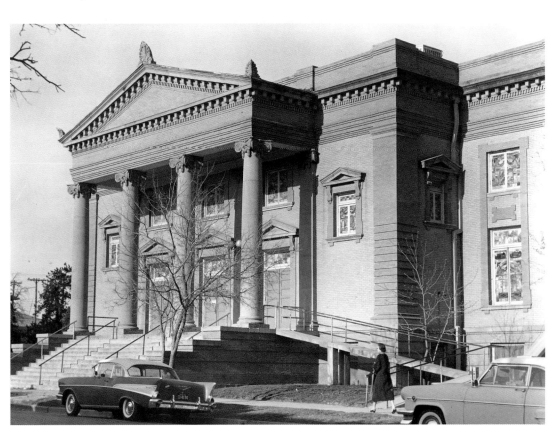

The church's outreach to the community began in 1891 by its involvement in the establishment of Simmons College (later Hardin-Simmons University). In 1892, the church established its first mission, Oak Street Mission, in a laundry building. This mission became South Side Baptist Church in 1908. Valley View Mission (which became Calvary Baptist Church) followed in 1906 and Walnut Street Mission (later Immanuel Baptist Church) in 1908. The Mexican Mission (later First Mexican Baptist Church) began in 1909. As the church continued to grow, it started Sunset Mission (later Elmwood Baptist Church) in 1931, Cherry Street Mission in 1949, Sears Addition Mission (later Ambler Baptist Church) in 1951, Elmwood Baptist Mission in 1953 (which became Pioneer Drive Baptist Church in 1955), and Lytle South Mission (which became Lytle South Baptist Church) in 1987. The church's present mission efforts include Templo Bautista and City Light Community Ministries. A twenty-year-old television ministry reaches out to the Big Country and northern New Mexico.

The Reverend Bennett Hatcher became the first permanent pastor in November 1883, beginning a distinguished line of pastors. Dr. Millard A. Jenkens served the longest tenure, from 1915-1948. He was followed by Dr. Jesse J. Northcutt (1948-1949), who then joined the faculty of Southwestern Seminary; Dr. James L. Sullivan (1950-53), who left to become president of the Baptist Sunday School Board; and Dr. Elwin L. Skiles (1953-1966) who became president of Hardin-Simmons University. Dr. James Flamming (1966-1983), who then became pastor of the First Baptist Church of Richmond, Virginia, followed Dr. Skiles. Dr. Bill G. Bruster (1985-1994) accepted an administrative post with the Cooperative Baptist Fellowship, which he had helped to found. Dr. Philip L. Christopher, the church's present pastor, began his ministry here in 1995.

The church's mission statement, "to reach people for Jesus Christ and help them become more like Him," has been a guiding force in bringing First Baptist to this point in history and will lead it into the next century.

An illustration of the First Baptist Church expansion of 1954 at 3rd and Orange Streets.

KEAN 105

KEAN…the station that says a lot for Abilene, is one of the oldest country radio stations in America, and one of the first to broadcast on the FM dial. After starting as a rock and roll station known as KNIT, it jumped on the country bandwagon in 1978, and never looked back.

Every year for the past twenty-one years, KEAN's audience has made it number one in the city. Few, if any radio stations in the country can claim these bragging rights. KEAN's massive audience is so loyal that the station often has the highest audience share of any station throughout the United States in any format.

The station has been nominated five times in the past nine years for "Station of the Year" by the Country Music Association and won the award in 1987. It's been nominated twice and won one "Marconi" award from the National Association of Broadcasters.

KEAN's national reputation for artist development, listener loyalty, and community service has literally put Abilene on the radio map. Mention KEAN anywhere in the U.S. and country listeners will say, "Oh, yeah, KEAN 105, Abilene, Texas." KEAN 105 decals have been seen on New York taxis, Philadelphia trucks, on the bows of ocean-going vessels, and during the 1998 emergency action in Iraq, on the foot lockers of personnel headed for the Persian Gulf.

When it comes to compassion, KEAN and its listeners is an unsinkable lifeboat of hope, raising thousands of dollars for good causes.

KEAN made national headlines during 1995's devastating drought, when farmers and ranchers in Alabama and Georgia were desperately in need of hay. The station orchestrated a massive hay drive that culminated in nineteen train carloads of hay shipped to the beleaguered farmers. Later, Texas Secretary of Agriculture Jim Hightower presented KEAN with the state flag that flew over the train cars.

KEAN was first on the scene with a fund drive after the Cross Plains tornado and a fund drive for the victims of the Oklahoma City bombing; and has raised millions of dollars for causes from the Food Bank to drug awareness programs to the March of Dimes.

By agreeing to be frozen in a block of ice for forty-eight hours, KEAN air personality Rudy "Fearless" Fernandez raised over 65,000 pounds of food for the Food Bank. He was also suspended eighty feet in the air in a van—twice—and buried alive in a casket, raising over $45,000 for various causes. (No wonder they call him "Fearless"!)

The KEAN Big Bass Bonanza, begun by the station in 1978, is the second largest amateur bass fishing tournament in the world drawing participants from as far away as Canada. This tournament has yielded $1.5 million in prizes.

For seventeen years, KEAN has staged an annual Cruise Night inviting Texas car clubs and KEAN listeners to join in fun for the entire family. Cruise Night features sanctioned drag racing, car competitions, prizes for the best costumes, and a sock hop with a country band playing '50s oldies.

The KEAN Tax Relief Day party has become a major annual event in downtown Abilene. KEAN goes on location at the downtown post office every year of April 15 (the 105th day of the year) for Tax Day Relief, handing out PayDay candy bars, free pizza and sodas, while massage therapists offer taxpayers tension relief.

From humble beginnings with a handful of employees on the eleventh floor of the Windsor Hotel to a national reputation as a leading radio station, KEAN never takes listener loyalty for granted, and it always reminds us that "ABILENE IS KEAN."

Above: Brooks and Dunn greet lucky KEAN winner.

Below: KEAN Big Bass Bonanza, second largest amateur bass fishing tournament in the world.

FIRST INDEPENDENT COMPUTERS, INC./ COLUMBIA CAPITAL CORPORATION

First Independent Computers, Inc./Columbia Capital Corporation is a fine example of how the American enterprise system works. This company, born in answer to a need for a specialized service, has grown by concentrating on a niche market of three services: Credit and Debit Cards, Banking and Financial Services, and Document Management and Distribution.

First Independent Computers, Inc. (FICI) began in 1968 as Data Processing Center (DPC), a division of First State Bank of Abilene, to process the bank's financial records. Soon several other Abilene banks began outsourcing their financial records processing to FICI.

In 1983, DPC was incorporated, changed its name to First Independent Computers, Inc., and became a subsidiary of First Independent Bank Shares, Inc.

From 1987 to 1997, FICI continued to do well as a business while its common stock went through a series of ownerships until 1997, when Columbia Capital Corporation acquired the company as its wholly-owned subsidiary.

Officers of Columbia Capital include Kenneth A. Klotz, chairman of the board of directors and president; Olan Beard, vice president and director; Charles LaMontagne, chief financial officer, secretary and director; Robert M. Feldman, director and Donald L. Thone, director.

By providing data management services to small to medium-size companies such as small banks, credit unions, insurance companies and others without the resources to operate their own in-house programs, FICI functions as a vital link between these organizations and their customers. Thus capturing the initial transaction at the point of sale, crediting the merchant, posting the transaction to the bank's ledger, and posting it to the customer's statement.

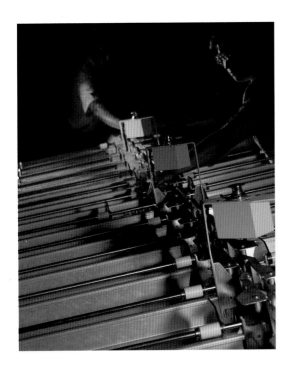

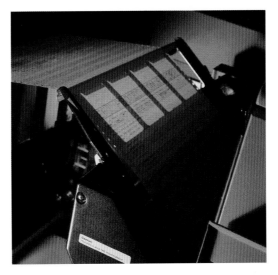

FICI assumes all responsibility for processing systems, software maintenance and compliance. With a data processing center staffed around the clock, the customer has constant support available from his/her own Client Support Specialist. The company also provides 350 different special reports, which can be issued at the customer's request.

The company also offers "backroom" services and support, utilizing special software to access the three major credit bureaus and score applicants' credit applications.

Backroom service also provides fully-automated and personal customer service support for credit card holders, who may activate their cards, verify account information and report lost or stolen cards.

Another service offered by FICI is credit and debit card production and embossing. Card production services include, in addition to the customary embossing, magnetic stripe encoding and printing, the printing capability of signatures and fingerprints, and Smart Card Personalization.

The Document Management and Distribution Services arm of the company provides data management solutions to such overwhelming problems of document distribution, reducing the flood of paper, as well as the cumbersome and time-consuming metering and mailing operation. The company processes over one million pieces of mail per month, and is ranked as one of the fastest growing First Class mailers in

the Fort Worth Regional District by the U.S. Postal Service.

All this is done while FICI continues to stress a personalized, customer service-oriented approach to its customers, giving those companies who have outsourced their accounts the assurance that the individual credit card holder will remain a satisfied buyer.

As the world continues to rapidly move toward electronic information processing, annual credit/debit card purchases in the U.S. have reached the $1 trillion mark and continue to increase. The combination of this type of growth and the continuing general trend toward outsourcing data processing functions continues to benefit the company. With the company's short but storied history in Abilene, the road ahead looks to be a journey of success into the future.

HANNA LAW FIRM, L.L.P.

The roots of the Hanna Law Firm first took hold in Abilene in 1961 with Bob Hanna returning to Abilene from the City Attorney's office in Lubbock, Texas. Hanna had first come to Abilene in 1950 from the cotton fields of Turkey, Texas, to attend Hardin Simmons University. After graduating from Hardin Simmons University in 1954 and intervening service in the United States Army, Hanna attended and graduated from Baylor University Law School in 1960.

Along the way, Hanna has been associated with several distinguished and outstanding Texas lawyers including: Malcolm Schultz, Tom Webb, Aubrey Stokes, Jim Robinson, Sam Moore, W. L. (Dub) Burke, the Honorable Jorge Solis, the Honorable Jess Holloway, and the Honorable John Weeks.

Hanna has been a member of the State Bar of Texas since 1960 and is honored to practice before the U.S. Court of Appeals for the Fifth Circuit and the U.S. District Courts for the Northern, Western, and Southern Districts of Texas. He became certified by the Texas Board of Legal Specialization in Personal Injury Trial Law in 1978, the first year such certification was offered.

Jon Hanna grew up in Abilene, Texas, attending Abilene schools, graduating from Cooper High School. He received his undergraduate

degree from the University of Texas at Austin in 1979 and studied law at Texas Tech University, graduating in 1982. Jon Hanna joined Bob after his graduation and they have practiced law together ever since. In addition, Jon has served the State of Texas as a special prosecutor and as Special Counsel to the State Bar of Texas.

Top: Bob Hanna (left) and Jon Hanna.

PHOTOGRAPHS COURTESY OF MORRIS STUDIO.

The building housing the Hanna Law Firm is part of Abilene's history. It has been the home to one of Abilene's early boarding houses, two grocery stores, and a blacksmith shop. Renovation of the building in the early '70s received the Frank Grimes Beautification Award.

Although originally engaged in the general practice of law, by the early 1980s, the Hanna Law Firm was dedicated solely to the representation of injured citizens. In the course of these efforts, they have preserved and defended the rights of the injured and fought powerful corporations on behalf of working men and women and their families. Representative cases arise out of industrial accidents, specifically relating to the oil field industry, occupational injuries, motor vehicle accidents, nursing home neglect, and professional malpractice. Over the years, they have also handled cases involving defective products, toxic pollutants, and chemical exposure.

To facilitate the handling of complex litigation and its client volume, the Hanna Law Firm has assembled an extraordinary group of dedicated and highly skilled legal assistants and support staff from Abilene and the surrounding area. Together, they work to service the needs of their clients and help make Texas and

Abilene a safe and responsible environment for our families. Outside the office, they have maintained a firm tradition of public service and philanthropy. The Hanna Law Firm is proud to be a part of the history of Abilene and West Central Texas.

ABILENE INSURANCE AGENCY

Abilene Insurance, a family business since it opened in 1965, in known for its quality service and integrity. Left to right are the company's family management team, daughter, Denise Yarbro Oliver, mother, Donna K. Yarbro, and son-in-law, Les Oliver.

Donna K. Yarbro, owner of Abilene Insurance Agency, got her start in the insurance business in 1965, filing Workman's Compensation claims and answering the phone. Insurance was a natural for the single mother, and she soon took on other jobs in the office, until she was in effect responsible for most of the agency's operations.

Then in 1984, she stepped out on her own, opening an agency with only her paycheck and a contingent of insurance companies who believed in her so strongly that they "planted" with her—allowing her to offer their insurance to her customers.

Donna was Abilene's only female sole proprietor independent insurance agent.

As Yarbro Insurance Agency grew, finding qualified help was easy for Donna, since her daughters, Dani and Denise, had both worked for her since their teens and liked the work. First Dani came to work for her, but later left to start a Farmers Insurance Agency. Then in 1988, Denise came into the business, and it remained a solely woman-run agency until 1997, when Denise's husband, Les Oliver, joined the agency.

Donna's son, Dean, is a radiologist in Las Vegas.

As the company grew, Donna changed the name to Abilene Insurance Agency in order to better reflect the scope of the business. Early on, oil industry insurance was a staple of her business, but as time went by, Donna began to look for niche markets. Now Abilene Insurance Agency writes transportation insurance for trucks, wreckers, dump trucks, etc. throughout Texas. Churches are another niche market that Abilene Insurance Agency fills, along with contractors, and most commercial insurance.

Both Donna and Denise are active in the Abilene Association of Independent Insurance Agents, where Denise has served as president and Donna as vice president.

"Abilene Insurance Agency has changed with the times and will continue to change," Donna says, with two important exceptions: "This will remain a family business, and we will continue to keep our customers' best interest always at the forefront."

"Currently, we are putting a special emphasis on auto and homeowners insurance" says Donna.

St. John's Episcopal School opened in 1952 as a private kindergarten with eighteen children enrolled, under the auspices of the Episcopal Church of the Heavenly Rest. Classes met in various parish buildings, and the kindergarten was called St. John's Day School.

One grade was added each year until the school had grown to include Kindergarten through sixth grade. In 1966, with more than 200 students, the school embarked on a building program. Through the generosity of Heavenly Rest parishioners and others in the community, St. John's built its own campus on donated property on South Bowie Drive, and moved into its new facilities in January 1967.

In 1983, the school moved once more to its present Sherman Street property, the site formerly occupied by Central Catholic High School. With room to grow, the school once again expanded, adding eighth grade and four-year-olds, with an all-day kindergarten.

But family needs and demographics were changing, and St. John's changed with them. The 1987-88 classes served four-year-olds through seventh grade. The next year, seventh grade was dropped, and in 1989-90, St. John's taught four-year-olds through fifth grade.

In 1990, classes for three-year-olds were begun. In 1991, enrichment classes became part of the total program and continue to be offered.

St. John's today serves 205 students (three-year-olds through fifth grade), with the emphasis on a strong classical approach to basics in learning while also offering a liberal arts approach with such enrichments as art, Spanish, physical education, computer science, and library science.

With a mission "To provide within a caring Christian environment an enriched academic program that emphasizes the development of each child's potential." St. John's needs only to look at its alumni, who have grown up to distinguish themselves both at home and far away, to see the success of this aim.

Top: First Grade at St. John's, 1953.

Below: Mrs. Burke's First Grade, 1999. First row (left to right): Connor Braaten and Rob Beckham. Second row (left to right): Caroline Dickey and Emma Morris. Third row (left to right): Matthew McLeod and Timothy MacArthur.

ARROW FORD, INC.

Since its inception in 1964, Arrow Ford has been a family-owned, hometown company. The company plans to be going strong into the twenty-first century, moving forward with the vision of its founders, the late H. S. "Higg" Higginbotham and his partner, Lynn Lee. In 1964, these two pioneers sat in the Walgreens Drug Store coffee shop in the old Westgate Shopping Center and started the business that is now Arrow Ford.

Above: The Arrow Ford facility today.

Bottom: The original Arrow Ford location, circa 1956.

In June 1964, Higginbotham and Lee purchased the Abilene Ford franchise from A. M. McIlwain. They christened the new dealership "Arrow" Ford and initially did business in the old McIlwain Ford building at 4241 South 1st Street.

Over the next ten years, Arrow Ford prospered and outgrew its physical plant. So in 1974, the partners purchased and remodeled the former Western Chevrolet facility at 4001 South 1st Street.

As the twenty-first century approached, Arrow Ford recognized the need for additional state-of-the-art facilities. Thus began the one-year renovation process that was completed in 1996. This renovation and upgrade enables Arrow Ford and its employees the ability to continue to provide the quality service and customer satisfaction that has been its trademark for over thirty-five years.

Since Arrow Ford's inception, a lot of things have changed around Abilene. For example, Westgate Center was demolished, taking with it that old Walgreen's drug store where Arrow was formed. The McIlwain building, Arrow's first home, was torn down and several other businesses now occupy that property.

Arrow's 165 employees have continued to serve Abilene with new and innovative ideas. For example, the dealership was the first to offer repair service on Saturdays, and the first to provide multiple used car locations, each designed to meet different customers' needs. When the Arrow Internet site went online, customers could check out the inventory of used cars by using their home computers.

Arrow also continues to be a family-oriented business. In the late 1970s, Lee sold his share of Arrow Ford to Higginbotham's three sons—Seaton, Dale, and Vinson—and Arrow became wholly owned by the Higginbotham family. H. S. Higginbotham died in 1995, and today, Arrow is still owned by his three sons. The business has become generational, as Higg's grandchildren have joined the work force and management team. Together, the Arrow Ford family still strives to carry forward Henry Ford's philosophy, which Arrow's founder adopted back in 1964—"to provide a quality product that everyone can afford."

Associated Publishing Company's roots have grown deep since Peter MacInnes moved to Abilene in 1977 and formed the new directory business. APC was a pioneer in a new field, created as the result of the divestiture of AT&T and this made the future of the industry uncertain at that time.

In 1978, the first Big Country Telephone directory was published. The directory provided more features and a wider range of listings than traditional telephone directories. The early directories typically combined the listings of several utility and telephone cooperative directories into one directory serving a well-defined retail trade area. The first edition to include Abilene was published in 1985. The Abilene directory had expanded the original coverage and features concept to include a telephone number and street cross-reference. During its first five years, APC operated with only three employees. By 1986, more than forty people worked at the 1052 North 5th Street location and its field branch in Midland.

Local investors purchased APC from Mr. MacInnes in the early 1990s. By that time, operations had expanded to include the Bryan-College Station and San Angelo areas. The Hearst Corporation, one of the nation's largest diversified communications companies with headquarters in New York City, acquired APC in 1994. Bob Allen III, vice president of operations and a graduate of Abilene Christian University,

was promoted to president soon after the acquisition.

"Hearst wanted to get into the yellow page business and their roots were already deep in Texas," Allen stated, referring to Hearst's ownership of the *Houston Chronicle* and *San Antonio Express-News* as well as several community newspapers in Texas.

By 1998, APC had increased its advertising revenues by more than five times in eight years and employed more than 100 people statewide. Corporate operations and all directory composition activities remained headquartered in Abilene during this remarkable growth phase. Currently, Area-Wide Phone Books are published for Abilene, the Permian Basin (Midland and Odessa), San Angelo, Laredo, Bryan-College Station, Heart of Texas (Brownwood, Brady), Plainview, Big Spring, Snyder, Colorado City, Sweetwater, Big Country East, and West of the Pecos.

Early in 1998, APC entered the World Wide Web, developing and maintaining the operation of three Internet sites for the Abilene, San Angelo and Bryan-College Station markets. The sites capitalize on local events, plus they offer web visitors local news, weather and sports including yellow and white page listings, information on apartments, real estate, movies, restaurants, and travel.

Consistent with its mission and culture statement, APC has been actively involved in civic and charitable activities in the communities it serves. "It is our intention to be a good corporate citizen as well as to encourage all our employees to become active players in our churches and community organizations. We want to be as good to the community as the local communities have been to us in using and in supporting our hometown area-wide directories," said Allen.

In 1999, Associated Publishing Company observed its twentieth anniversary. The company has satellite offices in San Angelo, Midland, Laredo, and Bryan, Texas.

APC publishes and distributes over 900,000 Area-Wide Phone Books to businesses and residents in ten Texas Markets covering seventy-seven counties and one million people. Membership includes Association of Directory Publishers and Association of Directory Marketing.

ASSOCIATED PUBLISHING COMPANY

Bob Allen III, president of Associated Publishing Company.

SENTER, REALTORS®

purchased an old grocery store at 2901 South 1st and remodeled it to accommodate up to fifteen real estate agents, plus an insurance and management business.

In 1969, Senter's first year in the remodeled building, it became the city's number one volume sales company, with total sales of more than $2.5 million.

With an emphasis on quality agents and first-class service, the company has remained a top volume real estate company in West Texas, with growth currently having surpassed $46 million in total sales annually. In May of 1995, Senter sold the South 1st properties and opened offices at 3401 Curry Lane at Winters Freeway.

❖

Top: (Left to right) Charles McKinney, Scott Senter, Bill Senter, Steve Senter, and Sydney Senter McKinney.

Bottom: .Senter, REALTORS® office at 3401 Curry Lane at Winter's Freeway.

Senter, REALTORS® began in 1957 when Bill Senter obtained his broker's license to complement his insurance agency, opened the year before. In 1962, Bill expanded the company and the initial office was located at 2925 South 1st.

In 1964, the company began to broker FHA-repossessed homes and Bill's father, Earl, retired from Shell Oil Company to become the company's FHA property manager. The company handled enough transactions to be a top company in town.

In the mid-1960s, when most real estate companies were small one- or two-agent firms, Bill, with a vision of Abilene's future growth,

All three of Bill and Lila Senter's children grew up in the business, cleaning offices, mowing lots, and other duties. Steve Senter is now a partner in CBS Insurance; Sydney is vice president of Chaparral Management Company; Scott is owner of Senter, REALTORS®; Steve Stovall and Charlie McKinney are vice presidents.

The Senters have a long history of community service, including serving on the boards of the Abilene Chamber, the Abilene Industrial Foundation, and the Abilene Board of Realtors, as well as supporting the United Way, Junior League, Pastoral Care and Counseling, Boy Scouts of America, and many other organizations.

Baack Florists, Nurseries & Greenhouses have been doing its part to keep Abilene beautiful for about sixty-five years, starting in the early 1940s with a small backyard operation in the Goodlow area belonging to Maxie Baack's mother, who grew flowers and plants to sell from her home. She found a ready market of eager homeowners. Soon her growing business enabled her and Maxie to move to a downtown store on Cypress Street.

Soon after moving downtown, Maxie and Erna Baack built greenhouses on Matador, where they offered high quality floral stock to an ever-growing number of customers.

They retired in the early 1970s and sold their business to a young Air Force captain who had a horticultural degree from Texas Tech University. Dan Harwell and his wife, Donna, had come from McCamey, but decided at the end of Dan's Air Force tour that they wanted to stay in Abilene.

In the twenty-eight years since buying Baack's, the Harwell's have expanded from a single store with three full time employees to four floral shops, a range of greenhouses, more than forty employees, and have added two nurseries, landscaping, and gifts to their growing line.

Baack's grows its own bedding plants and pot plants such as poinsettias, geraniums, Easter Lilies, hydrangeas, cyclamen, natives, and well-adapted flowers with exotics from as far away as Holland and Hawaii.

Dan Harwell attributes his success to the loyalty of his customers and the excellence of his employees.

"There are simply no words to express my appreciation for the people of Abilene," he said.

His motto is: "Doing business with a conscience void of offense toward God and Man, giving service to exceed our customer's expectations."

TOP PHOTO COURTESY TOM MILLER PHOTOGRAPHY.

Below: 10,000 pots of poinsettias.

BIBLE BOOK STORE

The Bible Book Store sits in the heart of Abilene, in the downstairs section of a residence built in 1924 on the strip of Butternut that for years was called "The friendly mile." It began in 1948 as the Victory Bible Center, owned and operated by the Pastor of the Abilene Bible Church, Dr. Joe Temple and his brother-in-law, Bernard Smith. Previous to that, there had been another bookstore inside the church, opened by the Zondervan Publishing Company to minister to the soldiers of Camp Barkley, but it was closed with the end of World War II.

In March, 1970, a young Air Force couple, Dan and Donna Harwell, stopped into the book store and bought two books, one for husbands and one for wives. In 1972, they moved their church membership to the nearby Abilene Bible Church, and they continued to purchase books from the Bible Book Store.

Then in 1980, Dan and Donna Harwell became co-owners of the store. Already a vital part of a spiritually healthy and Bible-literate community, the Bible Book Store continued to grow and prosper.

In 1985, the Harwells enlarged the store, converting the remainder of the house into offices, shipping and receiving areas, and a separate music department. Donna says Christian products have increased ten-fold both in quantity and quality since she and Dan first visited the store, with such audio-visual materials as Bibles on tape and CD, Christian fiction, sacred art, and other accessories created around scriptural references.

She said she still loves coming to work in the Bible Book Store.

"The Lord has sent us the best employees, and the best customers, and it's wonderful having a place like this to come to work."

CCC SUPPLY

This page is dedicated to the memory of Travis Cranfill, who exemplified the ideal of fairness and honesty, both with customers and employees, that CCC Supply strives for.

CCC Supply, Inc. started out as a small radiator repair facility known as Abilene Radiator Works, Inc., run by M. C. and Doc Cranfill. In the 1960s, they added other lines to augment their seasonal radiator repair business. In 1965, ARW became one of Abilene's first suppliers of bumpers and body fillers, thus laying the foundation for expansion.

M. C.'s son, Travis and his wife, Patsy, came into the business full-time in 1973, during a decade of continual expansion and diversification. The shop added more bumpers and body shop supplies such as sandpaper and fillers to an ever-growing customer base.

The supply business was soon out-performing the radiator business, and the Cranfills continued to diversify and grow in response to demand from customers. CCC Supply in 1976 added its first paint line, R-M Paints, followed in the 1980s by PPG Paints, making the company a fully operational paint, body and equipment supplier.

The business spun off the radiator shop in 1987, in order to focus more fully on garage and body shop supplies. The close relationship between garage and body shop industries opened the way for expansion. CCC Supply continued to grow, and in 1993 became a full-line distributor of A-C Delco parts.

Then in 1995, Travis Cranfill was diagnosed with pancreatic cancer—a cancer that the doctor predicted would take his life in less than a year.

With no time to waste, the Cranfills' son, David, joined the business. Travis stretched out the year to three. He died in 1998. Patsy still works with David in the business, which is still changing and thriving, with a hardworking staff dedicated to the philosophy of customer satisfaction, and they look forward to the day when they may welcome a fourth generation—David's son, Grayson, born in 1999—into the business.

ABILENE SALES, INC.

Abilene Sales was founded in 1967 by Frank Levens, whose aim was simple: his nuts and bolts company would sell only industrial products meant to last, and the customer would always come first. Three years later, his brother-in-law, T. L. King, became a partner in the business, and three years after that, a nephew, Pete Fischer, joined them as outside sales representative.

❖

Employees of Abilene Sales, Inc., January 1999.

In 1980, Pete Fischer became President and General Manager, and soon expanded the products to include industrial supplies. In 1983, an air-conditioned showroom was added for customer convenience. The Fischer's children,

Stephanie and Stephen, grew up in the business and learned that nothing is more important than a customer's satisfaction, or a customer's time.

"It is my philosophy that the customer can wait in line at other stores, but not at my store," Mr. Fischer explains.

At the end of its thirty-first year, Abilene Sales has thirteen employees and an inventory of mostly American-made products. Stephanie's husband, David Sullivan, has joined the company, and Stephen, who swept floors and packaged merchandise as a child, is now the owner of his own fastener company, Angelo Bolt and Industrial Supply, in San Angelo.

Mr. Fischer said employee selection is a very painstaking process.

"We're very proud of our employees, and have a very low turnover of personnel. Our benefit package is second to no other company in the area."

Johnny Watkins, head counterman, has been with the company twenty-two years. Another staff member, Hayden Harrell, is a fourteen-year employee, and Jeremy Dellasius came on board seven years ago.

Pete Fischer attributes the success of Abilene Sales to the loyalty of his customers, many who are second generation customers.

"We pride ourselves on doing right, with quality merchandise, and we want our customers to be totally satisfied with what they buy from Abilene Sales, Inc.," he said.

Abilene's Retail Merchants Association began in 1909 and was purchased by C. R. Pennington in 1926. Upon his death in 1971, the business passed to his daughter, Estha Neva Pennington Cockerell, and then on to her two sons, Carroll and Edward Cockerell. They bought the building at 1133 North 2nd and moved the business to its current location. Carroll has taken an active role in the business since 1976, while Edward is a practicing attorney. The business became known as the Credit Bureau servicing West Central Texas in 1976.

In the early days of credit reporting, information was typed on three by five index cards. When an individual wanted to obtain credit, the Credit Bureau received a telephone call. One of the twenty-five to thirty employees would pull the file and read it to the creditor. Urgent updates were received by telegram.

As the credit industry evolved, the Credit Bureau has expanded into the collection business, publishing a weekly public record bulletin, operating a check collection service, and a "Welcome, Newcomer" service. The Credit Bureau computerized in 1978, taking nine months to input the data, but years to actually "let go of the manual information." After computerization, the staff was reduced to the current fourteen employees. Through the primary Credit Bureau in eighteen counties, creditors can access credit information anywhere in the U.S. via computer, twenty-four hours a day.

As a family-owned business, four generations have participated in the day-to-day operations. Carroll and Edward both began working at the bureau while in their teens, doing everything from reading reports to creditors to gathering courthouse information. Carroll's son, Marc, worked at the bureau and Carroll's wife, Karen, and stepson, Jason Maxwell, are currently working at the bureau. Edward's three children—Carolyn Dods, Eddy, and Chris—have all been employed in some capacity by the bureau.

The Credit Bureau is dedicated to providing a valuable service to the community and the credit industry.

RETAIL MERCHANTS ASSOCIATION OF ABILENE

❖

The owners of the Credit Bureau of Abilene and their families, July 1999. Left to right: Carolyn Cockerell Dods, Kay Cockerell, Eddy Cockerell, Edward E. Cockerell, Chris Cockerell, Carroll R. Cockerell, Jason Maxwell, Karen Cockerell, and Marc Cockerell.
PHOTO COURTESY OF ROBERTS STUDIO.

FIRST NATIONAL BANK OF ABILENE

Abilene's oldest bank, First National Bank of Abilene (originally named Farmers & Merchants National) was founded in 1889 by General Fleming W. James.

The bank was housed in a former saloon until a more fitting facility could be constructed. James' son, Henry, who would later serve as the bank's fourth president, went to work at the new Abilene bank as its bookkeeper. He was seventeen.

The bank began with a capitalization of $50,000 to serve the city of 3,200 people and the farmers and ranchers in the surrounding area. By the end of the year, its clientele had made deposits of more than $33,000. Today, the bank has over $53 million in capital and $550 million in deposits.

In 1957, the bank's name was changed to First National Bank of Abilene to reflect its widely diversified clientele and services. As the bank's service options and customer base expanded, so did the need for additional delivery channels.

In 1960, the bank built the First National Bank Ely Building and a multi-level parking garage across the street. It further accommodated the driving public in 1981 with the construction of a seventeen-lane motor bank. In 1981-82, First National added four twenty-four-hour ATM locations in Abilene. Today that number stands at fifteen.

Throughout the 1980s and 1990s, First National has continued to expand through acquisition and development. In 1995, First National introduced the concept of "supermarket banking" to Abilene with the opening of a new location in the HEB Food Store. The addition of offices in the Wal-Mart Supercenter and United Supermarket have expanded the bank's overall office locations to seven.

First National Bank of Abilene is committed to offering Abilene and its surrounding community the finest in financial products, delivery systems, and personal service.

❖

Left: The Hardin Administration Building at Abilene Christian University, c. 1955. The Hardin Administration Building marked the main entrance on Campus Court and still serves today as the site of administrative and academic offices, as well as several large classrooms.

Below: The Biblical Studies Building, built in 1989 and accessible from Judge Ely Boulevard via Teague Boulevard, houses the college of Biblical Studies and represents the new eastern front door to the Abilene Christian University campus. The Tower of Light in the background is the tallest structure on "The Hill" and provides a landmark visible for miles.

Because of one man's vision, a Christian school in a dusty little town called Abilene became a reality in 1906. A. B. Barret, the school's founder and first president, journeyed through West Texas by horse and buggy to raise financial resources to open the doors. Everywhere he went, he found ready support for the school that eventually became Abilene Christian University.

Originally established in downtown Abilene, ACU was founded as Childers Classical Institute for elementary and secondary school students. It was called "Christian College" even before becoming a junior college in 1914 and a senior college in 1919.

The school's name was officially changed to Abilene Christian College in 1920. In a visionary move in 1929, a new campus was built on a hill overlooking the city from the northeast, including the grand Hardin Administration Building.

By the late 1990s, Abilene Christian University was prospering on a beautiful, tree-shaded campus of 208 acres, with more than forty buildings and a high-tech infrastructure. The Biblical Studies Building and Mabee Business Building formed a new "front door" facing Judge Ely Boulevard.

As the university's enrollment exceeded 4,600 students from all fifty states and sixty nations, the quality of the education began to receive national recognition. ACU offers 117 baccalaureate programs through its three colleges and nursing school, and thirty-five master's programs and a doctoral degree through the Graduate School.

Through the years, the school has produced more than 84,000 alumni, including winners of Emmy, Telly, Grammy, and Inventor of the Year awards.

As a teaching institution, ACU emphasizes a dynamic, personal relationship between professors and their students. ACU faculty and staff work together to give students the rare gift of helping them connect their maturing beliefs and values with their actions.

BLUE CROSS AND BLUE SHIELD OF TEXAS

❖

Above: Like many communities across Texas, the city of Gainesville proudly displayed that the entire town had enrolled as members of Blue Cross.

Below: With a work force of more than 650, Blue Cross' Abilene facility handles claims and customer service for 350,000 federal and 250,000 state employees, retirees and their dependents.

As Texas' first and largest not-for-profit health coverage provider, Blue Cross and Blue Shield of Texas provides coverage for more than two million customers, offering a full spectrum of individual health coverage and employee benefit programs.

In 1996, the company was searching for a new location for its Federal Employee Program claims and customer service operations. Abilene's strong work force, favorable real estate costs and community leaders' keen interest made Abilene a natural choice. The facility opened in early 1997 with great success. In fact, Blue Cross of Texas' decision to open a facility in Abilene proved to be so beneficial that the company later decided to house

claims and customer service for its Employees Retirement System of Texas contract there as well.

With a work force of more than 650, the facility handles claims and customer service for 350,000 federal and 250,000 state employees, retirees and their dependents. Blue Cross and Blue Shield of Texas looks forward to continued success in Abilene, just as it has throughout the state since its founding.

The story of how Blue Cross and Blue Shield of Texas opened the door to affordable health care for millions of Americans is a legacy handed down to us by one extraordinary man and his "50-cent" idea.

In 1929, Dr. Justin Ford Kimball, a former school superintendent, became an administrator at Dallas' Baylor Hospital and discovered the same problems he had faced as an educator.

Reviewing the hospital's unpaid accounts receivable, Dr. Kimball recognized names of many local schoolteachers. Knowing from experience that these low-paid teachers would never be able to pay their bills, he initiated the non-profit Baylor Plan, which allowed teachers to pay fifty cents a month into a fund that guaranteed up to twenty-one days of hospital care at Baylor Hospital.

The Baylor Plan—the genesis of modern health insurance—led to the creation of the organization today known as Blue Cross and Blue Shield of Texas.

Wagstaff, Alvis, Stubbeman, Seamster & Longacre, L.L.P. is the oldest law firm in Abilene and one of the oldest in West Texas. It is rich in history and tradition.

In July 1890, John M. Wagstaff left his position as president of the Buffalo Gap Presbyterian College to practice law in Abilene. He soon gained statewide recognition for his superior work as a trial lawyer, and his willingness to serve his community as a civic leader. The young Judge Wagstaff served as a State Representative in Austin. He helped celebrate the opening of Simmons College and was among the Abilene streetcar's first passengers. He attracted associates of like mind and the one-man law office grew to a partnership known for its integrity and industry.

The firm, from the very beginning, sank its roots deep in downtown, investing in the future of Abilene. John Alvis, another early partner, served as an Abilene City Commissioner, Hardin-Simmons University trustee, and commander of the State National Guard Battalion in Abilene during World War II. Bob Wagstaff, son of John M. Wagstaff, also served in the Texas Legislature and was instrumental in drafting water law legislation known as the Wagstaff Act. David G. Stubbeman was mayor of Abilene and member of the Texas Legislature. C. R. Dickinson became Judge of the Eleventh Court of Appeals sitting in Eastland, Texas. Longtime managing partner Robert H. (Bob) Alvis and numerous other partners have served as trustees and directors of many non-profit corporations, churches, and agencies, as well as on civic committees in service to the community.

Today, the Wagstaff law firm continues that tradition of excellence and service.

Wagstaff attorneys continue to serve the Abilene community, state and local bar organizations. The firm has supported the Grace Cultural Center, established a law scholarship for students, and invested in the redevelopment of Abilene's central business district with the purchase, expansion and renovation of its downtown offices, all while maintaining the style of law practice West Texans appreciate— one built on integrity, a strong work ethic and genuine concern for its clients.

WAGSTAFF, ALVIS, STUBBEMAN, SEAMSTER & LONGACRE, L.L.P.

❖

Top: John M. Wagstaff. Founded firm in 1890. Died 1952.

Left: Standing (left to right): John R. Saringer, Darrell W. Moore, Roy B. Longacre, Kyle D. Tatom, Charles L. Black. Sitting (left to right): Diann D. Waddill, Don N. Seamster.

PHOTO BY ROBERTS STUDIO.

BATJER & ASSOCIATES, INC.

In 1947, Arch Batjer and Ralph St. John began Batjer and St. John, a residential heating and air conditioning installation and maintenance service at 765 Hickory. As Abilene expanded, the company grew, and in 1951, they hired mechanical engineer, Frank E. Peck. This enabled the company to pursue commercial and industrial work. In 1955, they hired Lewis Chase.

Mr. St. John retired in 1957 and the company's name became Batjer and Associates. The partners included Arch Batjer, Frank E. Peck, Larry Purcell and Wiley Connally. In 1958, Jim Jennings came to work in sales and estimating. In 1960, they added a plumbing department, supervised by Jack Pursley. The payroll was twenty-five.

During the 1970s, Batjer and Associates projects stretched from Abilene to San Angelo, Midland, Odessa, and Sweetwater to Bay Town and Del Rio. In 1976, Arch Batjer died and Frank Peck became company president. Other partners included Lewis Chase and Jim Jennings. Clint Ferrell and Mike Denny joined the firm.

In 1979, Batjer and Associates began to work only on commercial and industrial projects. When Frank Peck retired in 1986, the partners included Jim Jennings, president, Lewis Chase, vice-president, Clint Ferrell, vice-president, and Mike Denny, secretary-treasurer. There were fifty employees.

Lewis Chase retired in 1989 and Clint Ferrell died in 1995. In 1997, Jim Jennings died leaving Mike Denny as president. Batjer and Associates relocated to 2825 Pine Street, in 1998, to accommodate eighty-nine employees. Office personnel include Mark Sutphen, Casey Curnett, Randy Morris, Pat Stephens and Debby Gryzwa, with supervisors James Tate over plumbing, Dennis Seelke over sheet metal, and Pet Escobedo over service.

Denny attributes the success of Batjer and Associates to the hard work and training of its loyal employees, who have for so long placed customer satisfaction as top priority.

AUSTIN KING, M.D. & FAMILY

Congratulations to the Abilene Preservation League on preserving our irreplaceable heritage. Our family plays a part in that heritage.

T. J. Austin was one of the first settlers in 1876. He served as Callahan County judge, and minister for the Christian Church. His son, B. J., moved first to Baird then to Abilene in 1921. A son, Harold, served as an officer in World War I, then came back and eventually became district manager of West Texas Utilities' Abilene area. He was instrumental in bringing Camp Barkeley to Abilene in World War II, which propelled the town to city status.

Harold and Helen Austin were mainstays of Abilene's early social institutions. Their daughter, Elizabeth Gene, married Irvin King, son of a New York-born father who had come to San Antonio as a World War I pilot trainee, and whose mother came from a five-generation South Texas ranching family.

Irvin and Elizabeth King moved to Pecos to introduce irrigation to cotton farmers. He was killed in an accident, and Elizabeth returned to Abilene with her two sons, Greg and Austin, and later married Coy Warren, son of a pioneer oil family. They still reside in Abilene.

Austin King graduated from Baylor College of Medicine in 1973. During his residency in otolaryngology in Houston, he met Susan Lewis, daughter of a prominent Houston family and director of nursing in the largest surgical complex in the Texas Medical Center. They married in 1976.

When Dr. King opened his practice in Otolaryngology in 1979, Mrs. King opened Elm Place Ambulatory Surgical Center. Later, Dr. King founded the West Texas Voice Institute at Abilene Christian University. His research has resulted in a book, videotapes, and research papers presented globally. He was elected President of the Collegium Medicorum Theatri, which is an international organization of laryngologists from around the world. He was also elected president of the Taylor- Jones-Haskell County Medical Society.

Susan King is also a singer, an actress, and a member of the Abilene Independent School Board and serves on numerous other performing arts association boards.

It is the wish of Susan and Austin King that their three children, Helen, Lewis, and Martha, will follow the family heritage with contributions to the dynamic and growing future of Abilene.

❖

Above: The Austin King Family: Martha, Lewis, Helen, Susan, and Austin.
PHOTO COURTESY OF BUTMAN PHOTOGRAPHY.

Left: B. F. Austin (right) in 1880. Photo was taken after a cattle drive.

ABILENE BOOKKEEPING COMPANY, INC.

Paul and Connie Patterson opened their bookkeeping and tax preparation business in 1958, in an abandoned Texaco station at North 5th and Grape. That first year they prepared 300 returns at fees as low as $3.00 each. Now, thanks to forty-two years of hard work and computerization, they can prepare and process 300 returns in a day.

The three Patterson children—Debbie, Paul III, and James—are all involved in the business serving many of the original customers along with the children and grandchildren of the older customers. Debbie is an IRS Enrolled Agent and is president and in charge of IRS Audits. Paul III manages a branch office named "Abilene Electronic Tax Service." James is manager of "Tax Express," the electronic filing service of Abilene Bookkeeping Company.

There is a fourth office located at 3136 South 14th. This office is managed by Tim Adcock, who is also an Enrolled Agent and became a full-time employee upon graduation from Hardin-Simmons in 1983.

The Lord blessed the business and it has grown with Abilene, being the largest tax preparation service of the Big Country during the 1960s, '70s, '80s, and '90s. Paul himself has personally prepared more tax returns over those forty years than anyone else in the Big Country.

After more than four decades of serving the community, Abilene Bookkeeping is known not only for its standards of excellence, but for its sense of humor. For years Abilene's downtown parades included Abilene Bookkeeping's black 1947 Cadillac hearse with a sign mounted on top: "TWO THINGS ARE SURE, DEATH & TAXES. WE CAN SOLVE YOUR TAX PROBLEM." In 1976, to celebrate the U.S.A. bicentennial, they painted the hearse red, white and blue.

For thirty years, the company's marquee high above the parking lot has spelled out words of encouragement, challenge, gratitude, and humor. Many have called or written a note of appreciation for a particular message. The sign is changed every Tuesday, and has attracted the attention of the *Abilene Reporter-News*, which has run pictures and stories about the sign. Once the paper showed the sign misspelling the word "tongue". The following Tuesday, the marquee bore a message thanking the "Repeater-News" for pointing out the error.

Abilene Bookkeeping has employed many college students who have moved on to become CPAs, bank officers, corporation executives, and some business owners—most all who are presently leaders in their church and community.

Sun Supply celebrated its seventy-fifth year of business in 1998—the oldest locally-owned electrical supply company in the Abilene area. With thirty-two employees, it concentrates on West Texas.

W. K. Jennings, Jr. came out of the Navy at the end of World War II and went into the electric business with a friend, Horace Holley. W. K., Jr. knew electricity, since his father and Uncle Walter had founded Jennings Brothers Plumbing and Electric in 1907. Jennings and Holly Electric Company bought out their main competitor, Star Electrical Company with the aid of W. K. Jennings, Sr., who came into the company as partner with an infusion of cash. With the purchase of Star, they changed the name to Sun Electric. Two years later, W. K., Sr. bought out W. K., Jr. and Holley. At that time, he took on another partner, his son, Leroy Jennings, who became the company's president when his father stepped down.

Jim Jennings, the youngest, joined as vice president in 1946.

"We did a very simple type of wiring called knob and tube work," he said. "We also did bigger jobs such as electrical work on the Wooten Hotel, the Alexander Building, and Hilton Hotel (later the Windsor)."

In 1946, Sun built the building on North 5th Street where it presently sits. The focus changed from contract work to wholesale electrical supply, and the company was renamed Sun Supply Corporation. Later, when Leroy Jennings, Jr. joined the company in 1954, flooring material was added to the wholesale inventory. Jim became president in 1976 when Leroy, Sr. died. Leroy, Jr. died in 1993 and Jim retired in 1994 at age eighty-seven. Robert Calk succeeded him as the first president outside the family.

The new president didn't rush to change what has worked well in the past. "We continue to do business with a West Texas mentality," he explained. "We're committed to honest and ethical dealings, promoting our customers' profitability along with our own."

SUN SUPPLY CORPORATION

VICTOR HIRSCH, M.D., F.A.C.P.

❖

*Above: Victor J. Hirsch, M.D.,
F.A.C.P., receives the Courage Award
from the American Cancer Society.*

*Right (left to right): John Hirsch;
Victor J. Hirsch, M.D., F.A.C.P.;
Sherry Hirsch; and Samantha Hirsch.*

Dr. Victor J. Hirsch chose medical oncology as his specialty after his mother died of breast cancer. He and his wife, Sherry, moved to Abilene in 1982 and opened the city's first oncology practice with one assistant and one nurse.

He came to Abilene with a vision for quality cancer care for patients and their families residing in Abilene and the Big Country area.

He helped to initiate Abilene's first hospice program and served as its medical director.

He was instrumental in the organization of the I Can Cope Program and he served on the Board of the American Cancer Society. Then in 1984, he was diagnosed with Hodgkin's disease. Texas oncology physicians came from Dallas to assist local doctors in caring for his patients, while he took time off for treatment. After the Hodgkin's was successfully brought into remission, Hirsch continued his practice with a difference.

"Cancer has made me a better doctor," Hirsch stated. "I was extremely fortunate and I remember what I went through every time I see a patient."

In 1993, he merged his office with Texas Oncology, P.A. Today, Abilene is served by two cancer centers, with a staff of four medical oncologists, one radiation oncologist, a pharmacist and sixty other employees.

In 1998, Hirsch received the adult courage award from the Texas Division of the American Cancer Society in recognition of his courage and contributions.

When he isn't working for cancer prevention and treatment causes, he can be found with Sherry, John and Samantha, often in the midst of community events. Many Abilene students who participated in summer softball, baseball and football programs in past years still refer to him as "The Team Doc." But to his many patients, Hirsch will always be referred to as "The Cancer Doctor."

The replacement of NationsBank signs with Bank of America in Abilene was a historic occasion in 1999, signaling the coming of money management options never before available, with links to banks from coast to coast and beyond. It began as Citizens National Bank, founded November 1, 1902 by attorney J. M. Wagstaff.

In the 1980s, Citizens National Bank, like most banks in the country, underwent a series of mergers and name changes. The bank's product base widened while it maintained its adherence to responsible stewardship and community service. Citizens National Bank became Interfirst, then First Republic, and later NCNB. In 1992, the bank took the name NationsBank, with a new red, white, and blue logo, to better reflect its character—a change heartily approved by customers.

In October 1998, the merger of NationsBank and Bank of America created the nation's first coast to coast bank, with $618 billion in assets and customer access around the world and around the clock.

Today, Bank of America leads the state in loans to Texans. It's a leader in loans to minorities in low to moderate income markets. It's the number one bank lender of small business loans in the U.S., and it serves more than two million Texas households, with a deposit market share in Texas of almost sixteen percent.

Bank of America's involvement in its communities is deep and wide, with Bank of America associates volunteering in churches, schools, non-profits, and community groups, and serving on boards and committees of non-profit and economic development organizations.

The sign change, begun first where NationsBank and Bank of America overlapped, generated more than $5 million in income for seventeen vendors contracted to manufacture or install the signs.

Bank of America customers now have more choices, more convenience and technology than ever before, with their bank providing international corporate financial services for business transactions in 190 countries and maintaining more than 1,400 twenty-four-hour ATMs in Texas alone.

John Combs, president of the Abilene center, said the bank continues to invest in Texas, and that Abilene has strongly benefited. The conversion to one brand, one company in Texas is a milestone in our efforts to make banking work for our associates, customers and communities in ways it never has before. "If our original shareholders were here today, they'd take a lot of pride in what we've become," he added.

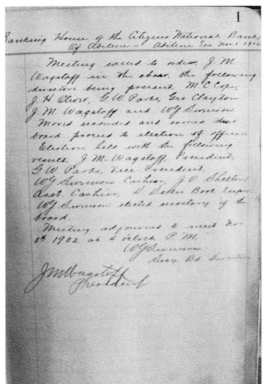

Left: J. M. Wagstaff, founder of Citizens National Bank.

Right: The minutes of the first meeting of the board of Citizens National Bank in 1902 signed by J. M. Wagstaff.

ROSE
BUILDERS, INC.

Top: Rose Builders' rehabilitation of the Windsor Building of the 1920s.

Below: The Rose-built 144,000 square foot Zoltek, Inc. processing facility.

Rose Builders, Inc. is a general construction firm with extensive experience in commercial construction, design/build and construction management. The firm operates primarily in the West Texas area, and it has credentials to operate in New Mexico.

It all began over seventy years ago, when Oscar Rose moved from the Indian Territory of Southeastern Oklahoma to work as a carpenter on an addition to a hotel in Abilene, Texas. That hotel still stands, and is now the Grace Cultural Building, a part of Abilene's downtown rehabilitation program.

With the completion of the Grace addition, Oscar Rose was contracted to build a portion of Camp Barkeley, an army-training base on the outskirts of Abilene. More military projects followed, and the Rose family began to expand outward, building in surrounding towns as their reputation for excellence grew. Many major buildings and fine structures throughout Abilene and West Texas carry plaques with the Rose name on them.

Oscar's son, Jim, presently runs the family business, which has more than $260 million in construction to its credit. Many of these projects were contracted by repeat clients who testify to Rose's reputation as a quality builder who always puts clients' needs first.

And now Jim's son, Jeff, has joined the firm to ensure the company will have a third generation of builders from the Rose family. Skill, integrity, and responsibility go into every phase of a building when the Rose firm is the builder.

"We are a proud family with tradition and we are happy to support any publication which touts our community and West Texas," said Jim Rose. "We believe Abilene is one of the most caring communities in Texas."

STENOGRAPH INSTITUTE OF TEXAS

Stenograph Institute was organized and continues to be operated as a private, post secondary educational institution dedicated to providing highly specialized training in court reporting, legal assistant/paralegal, legal secretary, medical secretary and related career fields. It is the foremost objective of the school to provide educational programs leading to clear and specific careers that are in high demand to assure ready employment of students upon graduation. The school is equally dedicated to assuring that the subject curriculum of each training program is relevant to current technology and professional practices to ensure the continuing adaptability and employability of its graduates.

The school is best known for its high academic standards and the success of its graduates. The court reporting alumni of Stenograph Institute includes several champions and finalists of state and national machine shorthand competitions; numerous officers and directors of regional, state, and national court reporter associations and various other professional organizations; many ownership principals and senior partners of private court reporting agencies and firms throughout the nation; and many holders of the coveted Registered Merit Reporter, which is one of the highest achievements awarded to court reporters by the National Court Reporters Association.

Stenograph Institute of Texas was originally founded in 1954 by H. Don Rodgers, CSR, RPR. Having first received his professional training in Washington, D.C., Rodgers had established a private freelance court-reporting agency in Abilene serving all of West Texas. As the demand for court reporting services outgrew the capacity of his agency, the need for additional professionally-trained court reporters gave rise to the establishment of Stenograph Institute, making it the oldest school of court reporting in continuous operation in Texas.

Top: Congressman Charles Stenholm speaks to the student body.

Left: H. Don Rodgers instructs court reporting students in the Alexander Building.

ABILENE TEACHERS FEDERAL CREDIT UNION

After almost half a century of serving educators and administrators, the Abilene Teachers Federal Credit Union is now a huge, friendly presence, with more than 19,000 members in sixteen counties, and over $123 million in assets.

President H. A. Dunn called the first board meeting, on October 18, 1950, with J. L. Sherman, Selma Bishop, W. P. Palm, and Willie Floyd also in attendance. Membership dues were twenty-five cents, and the Credit Union was run part-time out of a desk drawer.

In 1953, the Credit Union declared its first dividend—3½ percent. In November 1954, ATFCU made its first investments, putting $3,000 each into Abilene Savings and Southwest Savings at three percent. By 1963, assets had reached $1 million.

From 1967 through 1970, ATFCU added seven counties, McMurry College (now McMurry University) and Hardin Simmons University to its membership. The Credit Union, overflowing its assigned offices in the administration building, rented space in the Senter building on South First Street in 1969.

In 1972, real estate loans were approved. The Credit Union began a credit card program in 1978, with operations through a bank owned by credit unions, Town North National Bank in Farmers Branch, shortly after ATFCU moved into its own building in 1977.

The financial industry's S&L problems of the 1980s benefited credit unions everywhere. By 1985, ATFCU had 10,202 members, with assets nearing $40 million. IRA accounts were approved in 1981.

The Credit Union went online in 1981, and ATMs were approved for use in 1982. A branch

office opened on the south side at 2555 Buffalo Gap Road in 1988.

Today, the Abilene Teachers Federal Credit Union stands almost 20,000 strong, with deposits of over $107 million. A new eight-lane drive-through opened in May of 1997, and the location at 2801 North 6th, which was built in 1977, underwent major renovations in late 1998 and early 1999.

Abilene Teachers Federal Credit Union's only purpose is to serve its members. With its superior financial rating and strong field of membership, the credit union will continue for years to come, to fulfill the credit union motto, "Not for Profit, but for Service!"

BIBLIOGRAPHY

PRIMARY SOURCES:

Documentary Sources:

"Abilene Public Library Celebrates Abilene's Centennial." Abilene, Texas, 1981.

"Abilene Trade Guide and City Directory." Abilene, Texas: Magnetic Quill Book and Job Office, 1884.

Bluebonnet Brigade Collection, Tracy Shilcutt, Abilene Texas.

Cassagneres, Ed to Ms. Ruby Perez, Abilene Preservation League, February 20, 1996.

Historical Marker Files, Taylor County Historical Commission.

Minutes of the Board of Directors, Abilene Chamber of Commerce, 1926-1957.

"Our Homes and County Illustrated." Abilene: Chambers and Anderson, 1903.

"West Texas Today." West Texas Chamber of Commerce, May 1930.

Camp Barkeley PMGO Records, RG 389. National Archives.

Autobiography:

Frank Fujita, *Foo: A Japanese-American Prisoner of the Rising Sun*. University of North Texas Press, 1993.

Oral Interviews:

ALPS Oral History Project, Grace Museum, Abilene, Texas.

Bluebonnet Brigade Oral Interview Project, Tracy Shilcutt, Abilene, Texas.

McMurry History Interview Project, Grace Museum, Abilene, Texas.

Articles:

"The Abilene & Southern Railway Company." *Journal of Texas Shortline Railroads and Transportation*

vol. 2, no. 1 (Summer 1997).

McCombs, Holland. "The Army Pulls out of Abilene." Life, May 1945, p. 16-21.

Morrison, Madge. "We Have an Army Camp." *Atlantic Monthly* 168, no. 4 (October 1941): 501-502.

Savage, D. Keith, DDS, MA. "Early Record of Big Country Dentistry." *West Texas Historical Association Year Book* vol. LXXIV (1998): 85-91.

Savage, D. Keith, DDS, MA. "Hal Harrison Ramsey: Pioneer Texas dentist of the Big Country." *Journal of the History of Dentistry* vol. 46, no. 3 (November 1998): 103-109.

Newspapers:

Abilene Reporter News.

Camp Barkeley News, February 1942 to February 1945.

Taylor County News.

Yearbooks:

The Cactus, Abilene Christian High School, Abilene, Texas.

The Flashlight, published by the students of Abilene High School, Abilene, Texas.

SECONDARY SOURCES:

Dissertations and Theses:

Eoff, Shirley M. "Abilene, Texas, 1888 to 1900: A Town Striving for Success." M.A. Thesis, Hardin-Simmons University, 1978.

Gallaway, Steven Kent. "A History of the Desegregation of the Public Schools in Abilene, Texas, During the Wells Administration, 1954-1970." Ed.D. Dissertation, Texas Tech University, 1994.

Hatcher, John Henry. "A History of Dyess Air Force Base in Its First Decade: A Study in Community Relations." M.A. Thesis, Hardin-Simmons University, 1963.

Kincaid, Naomi. "The *Reporter News* and its Development of the Abilene Country." M.A. Thesis, Hardin-Simmons University, 1945.

Marler, Charles H., "Abilene Editor: Frank Grimes and West Texas." Ph.D. Dissertation, University of Missouri, 1974.

Myers, James M. "World War II an an Instrument of Social Modernization: The Social and Economic Influence of Camp Barkeley on Abilene, Texas." M.A. Thesis, Hardin-Simmons University, 1981.

Porterfield, Robert G. Jr. "The Early History of Abilene Up to 1920." M.A. Thesis, Hardin-Simmons University, 1969.

Shilcutt, Tracy McGlothlin. "The Bluebonnet Brigade: Women and War in Abilene, Texas: 1941-1945." M.A. Thesis, Abilene Christian University, 1993.

Tate, Curtis W. "Abilene's Golden Era: The Emergence of a West Texas City During the 1920s." MA Thesis, Hardin-Simmons University, 1991.

Turner, Karen Anderson. "Abilene at the Beginning of the Twentieth Century: An Analysis of the United States Census." M.A. Thesis, Abilene Christian University, 1989.

Books:

Abilene Reporter News. Abilene Remembered: Our Centennial Treasury Book, 1881-1981. Abilene, Texas: Abilene Reporter News Publishing, 1981.

Abilene, Texas: Preservation Plan and Survey/1979, prepared by Beasley and Welborn Preservation/Planning Consultants. Abilene, Texas: City of Abilene, 1979.

Allen, Frederick Lewis. *Only Yesterday: An Informal History of the 1920s*. New York: John Wiley and Sons, 1931.

Bowen, Oscar Kimsey. *Mr. Hendrick: Rancher, Oilman, Philanthropist.*

Carson, Julia M. H. *Home Away from Home*. New York: Harper and Brothers, 1946.

Casey, Clifford. *A Baker's Dozen*. Seagraves, Texas: Pioneer Book Publishers, Inc., 1974.

Cosby, Hugh. *History of Abilene*. Abilene, Texas: Hugh E. Cosby Co., 1955.

Downs, Fane, ed. *The Future Great City of West Texas—Abilene: 1881-1981*. Abilene, Texas: Rupert Richardson Press, 1981.

Duff, Katharyn. *Abilene... on Catclaw Creek*. Abilene, Texas: The Reporter Publishing Co., 1969.

Dyess, Wm. E. *The Dyess story*. New York: GP Putnam's Sons, 1944.

Fuller, James David. *Gunfire on South Front: History of the Abilene Police Department, 1881-1993*. Abilene Texas: Chaco Publications, 1993.

Gard, Wayne. *The First 100 Years of Texas Oil and Gas*. Dallas, Texas: Texas Mid-Continent Oil and Gas Association, 1967.

Halberstam, David. *The Fifties*. New York: Villard Books, 1993.

Hartmann, Susan M. *The Homefront and Beyond: American Women in the 1940s*. Boston: Twayne Publishers, 1982.

Hirshon, Stanley P. *Grenville M. Dodge: Soldier, Politician, Railroad Pioneer*. Bloomington: Indiana University Press, 1967.

Hutto, Homer H., ed. *Abilene: "The Athens of the West"*. Abilene, Texas, 1926.

Lack, Paul D., Robert W. Sledge, Fane Downs, and Paul E. Jungmeyer. *The History of Abilene: Facts and Sources*. Abilene, Texas: McMurry College, 1981.

Levering, Ralph B. *The Cold War: 1945-1987*. Arlington Heights, Illinois: Harlan Davidson, 1988.

Lingeman, Richard R. *Don't You Know There's A War On?: The American Home Front, 1941-1945*. New York: GP Putnam's Sons, 1970.

Pritchett, Jewell G. *The Black Community in Abilene*. Abilene, Texas: Pritchett Publications, 1984.

Richardson, Rupert Norval. *Famous Are Thy Halls: Hardin-Simmons University As I Have Known It*. Abilene, Texas: Abilene Printing and Stationery Co., 1964.

Spence, Vernon Gladden. *Colonel Morgan Jones: Grand Old Man of Texas Railroading*. Norman, Oklahoma: University of Oklahoma Press, 1971.

Steward, Hal D. *Thunderbolts: The History of the Eleventh Armored Division*. Nashville: The Battery Press, 1948, 1981.

Texas and Pacific Railway Company. *From Ox-teams to Eagles: A History of the Texas and Pacific Railway*. Dallas, Texas, 1945.

Wishcamper, Ed N. *From Tent to Computers: 100 Years with The Abilene Reporter-News, 1881-1981*. Abilene, Texas: The Abilene Reporter-News, 1981.

Zachry, Juanita. *Abilene: The Key City*. Aibilene, Texas: Windsor Publications, Inc., 1986.

Zachary, Juanita. *The Settling of a Frontier: A History of Rural Taylor County*. Burnet, Texas: Nortex, 1980.

Internet Sources:

Handbook of Texas Online. <http://www.tsha.utexas.edu/handbook/online/articles>

Unpublished Papers:

Downs, Fane. "History of the Abilene Public Schools." speech to Leadership Abilene, 1984.

Ganey, Madge .M. "History of the Abilene Carnegie Library, 1899-1955."

Hatcher, John J. "Seminar Report on the Military Background of the Abilene Country." Hardin Simmons University, 1963.

Lack, Paul D. " A Sense of Community: Beyond the Frontier Heritage." An Historical Perspective on Abilene, Texas, 1990.

Lack, Paul and Gerald McDaniel. "Did the Jazz Age Come to Abilene?" paper delivered to the West Texas Historical Association, Abilene, Texas, March 1979.

Men and Women in the Armed Forces from Taylor County, 1946.

Polk, Jim. "The History of Abilene and Taylor County." Texas Technological College (nd).

Vertical files at APL, McM, and ACU libraries.

INDEX

SPONSORS